# Snake Wilderness

### by Boyd Norton

**Sierra Club**  **San Francisco • New York**

For my mother, Edith Norton;
for love of wild and beautiful things.
Some of it rubbed off.

The Sierra Club, founded in 1892 by John Muir, has devoted itself to the study and protection of the nation's scenic and ecological resources—mountains, wetlands, woodlands, wild shores and rivers. All club publications are part of the nonprofit effort the club carries on as a public trust. There are 43 chapters coast to coast, in Canada, Hawaii and Alaska. Participation is invited in the club's program to enjoy and preserve wilderness everywhere. Address: 1050 Mills Tower, San Francisco, California 94104; 373 Fifth Ave., New York, N.Y. 10016, or 324 C Street, S.E., Washington, D.C. 20003.

This book is printed on Valentine Precycle Offset. The paper is manufactured from a nonwood fiber called bagasse. Bagasse is the residue that remains after sucrose has been extracted from sugar cane. The environmental benefits of using Precycle Offset are multiple: bagasse traditionally is burned (causing air pollution) or used for landfill in the wetlands of the Southeast.

Library of Congress catalog card number 78-189964.
International Standard Book number 87156-061-5.

Designed and produced by Charles Curtis, Inc., New York. Typeset in 11 point Times Roman on 13 points and printed in the United States of America by the Vail-Ballou Press, Inc.

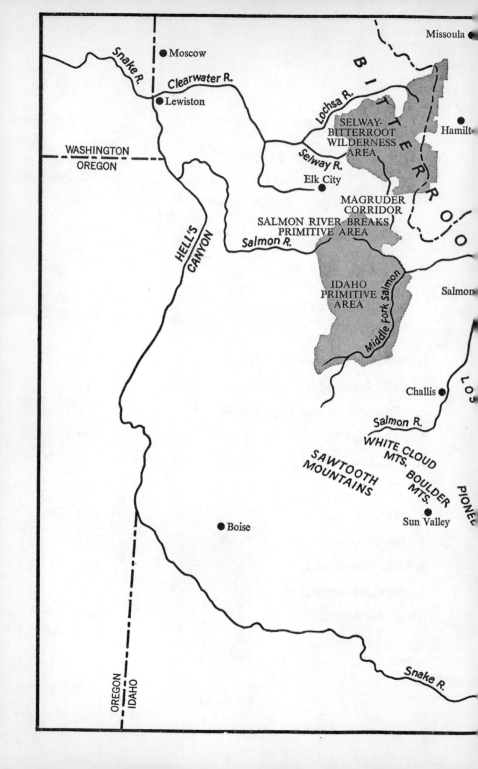

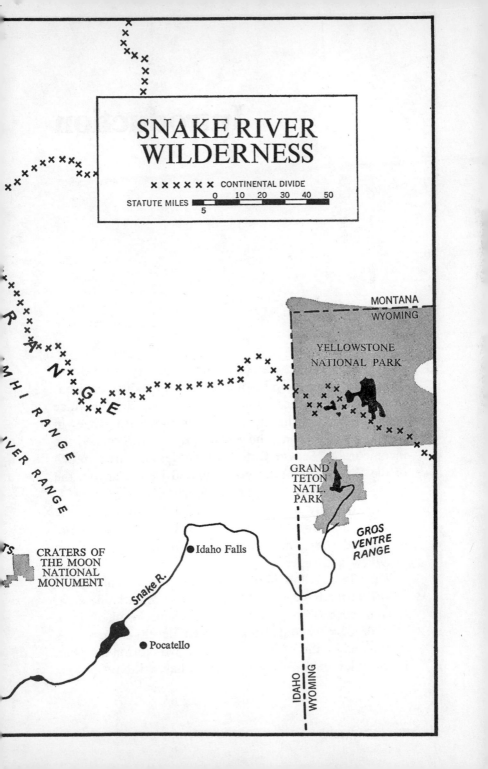

# SNAKE RIVER WILDERNESS

× × × × × × CONTINENTAL DIVIDE

STATUTE MILES

| 0 | 10 | 20 | 30 | 40 | 50 |

5

MONTANA

WYOMING

YELLOWSTONE NATIONAL PARK

R A N G E

MHI RANGE

VER RANGE

GRAND TETON NATL. PARK

GROS VENTRE RANGE

TS

CRATERS OF THE MOON NATIONAL MONUMENT

● Idaho Falls

Snake R.

● Pocatello

IDAHO

WYOMING

# Introduction

Idaho's Snake River watershed—the country of this book —rightly can claim to be one of the least spoiled environments in the United States. In addition, this province contains some of the most dramatic mountain ranges in the West (the Tetons, the Sawtooths, the Wallowas), the incomparable Selway-Bitterroot wilderness area, much of the Yellowstone back country, and Hells Canyon, the deepest gorge on the planet. Snake River country is unique in many ways: few, if any, large regions in the 48 contiguous states contain more wilderness areas, more unpolluted rivers, more memorable mountains, or more unsullied landscapes.

This Sierra Club book might be called a battlefield report on the besieged resources of this remarkable area. Classic conservation controversies have resulted in a number of pitched battles between development forces and the advocates of preservation. Boyd Norton has been in the thick of these fights, and he has written a powerful, partisan exposition of the issues. He recognizes that, to a substantial degree, the resolution of these disputes over dams, mineral resources, logging and new national parks will decide the long term environmental future of this region.

As a participant in the early stages of some of these controversies, I had a first-hand opportunity to evaluate the arguments of the antagonists. In those days, these disputes were regarded as "local," of primary concern only to the people of Idaho. Today, they are national issues. I believe this is a gain for the cause of conservation because each U.S. citizen, wherever he lives, is a co-owner of the national resources of the Snake River country.

When I became Secretary of the Interior twelve years ago, the dominant conservation idea in the Snake River valley (and the rest of the West) was what was then called "comprehensive development." The chief proponents of this policy, then and now, were the Army Corps of Engineers and the Bureau of Reclamation. A central assumption of these water planners was that the full "growth potential" of the region could be achieved only if a series of dams were built on every river. A corollary concept was that a region's mineral, timber and agricultural resources should also be developed to the maximum extent possible in order to fulfill the growth goals nurtured by development associations and chambers of commerce.

For good reasons, big dams have had a powerful grip on the minds of people in the Pacific Northwest. As the Columbia river was harnessed in the years following the building of Bonneville Dam, the abundant, cheap hydroelectric power produced at these huge dams transformed

the economic life of the region. However, ten years ago
few of us fully realized that even the Columbia River had
a limited number of prime damsites, and that once dams
were built at these locations subsequent plans for second-
and third-rate dams were bound to provoke controversies
with the outdoorsmen who prized these rivers for other
purposes.

Although growing numbers of these outdoorsmen were
skeptical of the long-term "benefits" of many resource
development projects, in the early 1960's most Idaho
conservationists felt powerless to stop the comprehensive
development juggernaut. Their ineptness was painfully
dramatized in 1961 when a last ditch effort to stop the
construction of Bruce's Eddy (now Dworshak) Dam on
the Clearwater got nowhere. It was also evident in the
fatalistic attitude of most conservationists that the full
reach of Hells Canyon was doomed to "full development."

A turning point came in 1962 when Sen. Frank
Church cast his lot with the conservationists (and risked
the wrath of Idaho mining, grazing, and timber interests)
by giving outspoken support to the Wilderness Act. And
the political climate was altered even more three years
later when Church elected to become the congressional
floor leader for a National Wild and Scenic Rivers bill
which put some of the finest tributaries of the Salmon and
Clearwater beyond the reach of the engineers.

Even though these landmark laws gained a foothold for
preservation concepts in the Snake River country, as the
1960's ended bitter controversies erupted over the "final
solution" for Hells Canyon, the future of the superb White
Clouds peaks, the status of the Sawtooth Mountains, and
the Forest Service's plans for logging the Magruder Corridor.

In 1972, to my mind at least, it is beyond argument that "comprehensive development" is an outdated doctrine. I believe the new environmental values which have won wide acceptance in recent years demand that certain broad principles govern whatever decisions are ultimately made concerning these resources:

- Now that ecological insight is part of our wisdom, we have a moral responsibility to pursue *optimum* solutions which will serve the long-term economic *and* environmental objectives of the nation.
- Everyone should acknowledge that these are not "local issues": the resources belong to all of the people, and, therefore, these issues must be resolved in appropriate national forums.
- As part of the decisionmaking process, all special interest groups must be forced to measure their goals and plans against the time-tested yardstick of the greatest good for the greatest number in the long run.

An admirer of his attitude toward resource problems once described Theodore Roosevelt as "a man with distance in his eyes." In deciding whether to dam, mine, log or otherwise develop the resources of the Snake River region, it is my own conviction that all of us will be more likely to make the right decisions if we approach them with "distance in our eyes" and place the rightful claims of the unborn alongside our own.

*Stewart L. Udall*
Washington, D.C.
September, 1972

# 1. The Land of the Snake

"Indeed, from all that we can gather from the journal before us, and the accounts of other travellers, who passed through these regions in the memorable enterprise of Astoria, we are inclined to think that Snake River must be one of the most remarkable for varied and striking scenery of all the rivers on this continent. From its headwaters in the Rocky Mountains, to its junction with the Columbia, its windings are upwards of six hundred miles through every variety of landscape. Rising in a volcanic region, amid extinguished craters, and mountains awful with the traces of ancient fires, it makes its way through great plains of lava and sandy deserts, penetrates vast sierras or mountainous chains, broken into romantic and often frightful precipices, and crowned with eternal snows; and at other times it careers through green and smiling meadows and wide landscapes of Italian grace and beauty. Wild-

ness and sublimity, however, appear to be its pre-
vailing characteristics."

Washington Irving

The view from the summit of Grand Teton is incredible.
High in this clear, cold air you can survey much of the
upper Snake River country: the Washakie and Gros
Ventre Ranges to the east; the Hoback and Wyoming
Mountains around to the south; the checkerboard farm-
lands of Teton Valley to the west, rimmed by the Big
Hole Range; and in the distant northwest, the Centennial
Mountain Range on the Montana-Idaho border. To the
north, of course, lies that sea of green forest called Yel-
lowstone.

This is where it all begins. At your feet, a dizzying
seven thousand feet below, the river is not many miles
old but already sizable, a silvery lacework threaded
across Jackson Hole. And in those soft blue and green
mountains to the northeast you can almost pick out the
spot where the river is born.

Officially, the origin of the Snake is an open grass-
covered divide somewhat lower than 10,000 feet located
near the southern boundary of Yellowstone National
Park. The divide is one of the most remote places left in
these lower forty-eight states: from this spot where melting snows spawn the great river, it is a minimum two
days' travel on any point of the compass to civilization.
Pick the wrong direction, and you might not even make it.

Actually, the Snake has many origins. It is not a single
trough of water rushing to the sea, but an interconnected
complex of streams and rivers, a system whose roots
extend deeply into the wilderness heartland of northwestern America. The little moss-lined spring above Alice

Lake in the Sawtooth Mountains is one of its beginnings. So, too, is Granite Creek, tumbling out of the Seven Devils Mountains, or Little Boulder Creek in the White Clouds, or Indian Creek in the Bitterroots, or any of a thousand other waters. The Snake is a vast web of water embracing a diverse multitude of life and land forms.

The main strands of that web are the Snake and Salmon and the Clearwater Rivers. Progressively smaller and nourishing these rivers are the Palouse, the Selway, the Lochsa, Grande Ronde, Imnaha and Payette, the Owyhee, the Boise, the Bruneau, the Big Wood, the Blackfoot, Henry's Fork, the Gray's, the Hoback, the Gros Ventre, the Lewis, and several score others. Beyond these the extensive structure becomes so fine as to defy any reasonable cataloging, and, geographers notwithstanding, that's just as well. In this world of magnetic memory cores and punched cards, what's needed is not more cataloging, but more understanding—understanding of the delicate relationship that exists between the life and the land defined by that fragile web.

Of course, you can't see it all from atop Grand Teton, high as its summit may be. More than one hundred thousand square miles are drained by the Snake River system, which embraces the largest chunk of unspoiled land this side of Alaska.

Almost six and a half million acres of fully protected, or reasonably well protected, wilderness lie within or touch the land of the Snake.* This number includes na-

---

* Lest I be accused of deception, let me point out that here I include *all* wild lands contiguous to those lying in the Snake River drainage. These figures include the whole wilderness in Yellowstone National Park, for example, even though only a part of the park actually lies in the Snake drainage. As another example, the total acreage for the Selway-Bitterroot Wilderness Area is included even though a stretch of some 200,000 acres

tional forest wilderness and primitive areas and those roadless portions of national parks and monuments likely to be added to the Wilderness System. Add to this a conservative two and a half million acres of de facto wilderness, lands currently without protective classification which are potential additions to the Wilderness System, and you have nine million acres of pristine lands lying in parts of Wyoming, Idaho, Oregon, and extreme northern Nevada—the Snake Wilderness—equal to the total acreage in the National Wilderness Preservation System when the Wilderness Act was passed in 1964. No one should forget, however, that it is also equal to less than a third of what we have put under pavement in this nation. Therein lies the problem.

Wildness and sublimity? Could Washington Irving see it today, he might have second thoughts about singing the praises of the Snake. Twenty-three dams already built or under construction blight the thousand-mile main stem of the river—roughly, an average of one dam every fifty miles. On the Snake's tributaries there are innumerable plugs as well, some small, some big, forty of them, probably. Maybe fifty. That "varied and striking scenery" has been altered by pavement, power lines, and pollution; those "green and smiling meadows" can nowadays deliver deadly doses of agricultural chemical runoff. Only a few places on the main Snake River can be characterized by the phrase "wildness and sublimity" any more. And still, not content with damage already inflicted, forces are at work to destroy even more of the area.

---

in the area overlaps the Continental Divide into Montana. My point is that this single geographical entity contains an immense amount of beautiful, unspoiled land.

This attack on the Snake Wilderness is taking many forms.

To the south of Jackson Hole, where the river leaves Wyoming through the impressive Snake River Canyon, the landscape is threatened by proposals for yet another dam. Once there is a lull in civic opposition, they'll be pouring concrete.

Fifty miles downstream the proposed Lynn Crandall Dam, a more imminent threat, would flood Swan Valley, a rural jewel of eastern Idaho. Although the project lies dormant for the moment, its advocates—the Bureau of Reclamation and huge farming corporations—are coolly waiting for environmental concern to pass.

The Teton River is the site of the most recent damming tragedy. This tributary of the North Fork of the Snake, fed by melting snows of the western flanks of the Tetons, has been celebrated in the journals of many early explorers. Today the Lower Teton Dam is a classic pork barrel project. When conservationists began to question its shaky justification, Idaho Representatives and Senators quickly ramrodded it through Congress before the public could discover its utter uselessness. The dam is authorized and funded. Only a last-ditch court action initiated by conservationists holds the bulldozers at bay.

On the North Fork of the Clearwater River, still another tragedy: the waters now rise behind the Dworshak Dam. Honest men would never have allowed those flood gates to close. The project pumped huge amounts of money into the local economy during construction, and that was, perhaps, ninety-five per cent of its *real* purpose. It should be allowed to stand with empty reservoir and unclosed gates, a symbol of man's stupidity and greed.

Mining menaces the entire Snake Wilderness. The

blade of the bulldozer is poised over the White Clouds and the Seven Devils. The lovely Lemhi Range is being scarred in an insane search for minerals. And a proposal to dredge mine the Snake near its source, where the river leaves Yellowstone and enters Jackson Hole, portends immense devastation in the shadow of the Tetons. Prospecting, dredging, claim staking continue unabated. There is no relief in sight from the tyranny of the 1872 mining law, a virtual carte blanche to exploiters of our mineral resources.

The whine of the chain saw, too, is becoming more and more prevalent where the wind once whispered through an unbroken forest. The U.S. Forest Service, passive protector of our trees, now supports those who would ravage them. Areas that could be added to the Wilderness System but may fall victim to Forest Service "management" include the Minam River country in Oregon, the upper St. Joe River, Clear Creek and Garden Creek, the Magruder Corridor in Idaho, and the western Tetons in Wyoming. Even the Idaho Primitive Area and the Salmon River Breaks Primitive Area are threatened by the agency's anti-wilderness tactics.

What dams, mines, and logging don't do, asphalt and concrete may. Hordes of motorized, aluminized tourists flock to Yellowstone-Teton country in increasing numbers, fleeing city pollution, ugliness, and crowding. Ironically, they threaten these unspoiled lands with the sheer volume of chrome and steel and asphalt. They may destroy the very beauty they seek.

But not all destruction is so clearly visible. The deterioration of water quality of streams and rivers, already reaching crisis proportions in a few places, forced the Idaho Department of Health to issue a warning against

eating fish caught in the middle and lower sections of the
Snake. The reason? High levels of mercury contamina-
tion. Moreover, nitrogen supersaturation of the water,
caused by all the dams on the Snake-Columbia system,
is now taking its toll among migrating salmon and steelhead. Extirpation of these species from the Snake and
Salmon rivers is a very real possibility.

The air deteriorates. In 1960 it was possible to see
clearly and consistently the magnificent Teton Range
from the desert country west of Idaho Falls. The sparkling
clarity of the air was a marvel. This view, once praised
by Washington Irving, is now a rarity. Today, when they
are visible at all, the Tetons are most often a hazy appa-
rition on the horizon, thanks mainly to a lumber mill in
St. Anthony, fertilizer factories in Pocatello, and increasing industrial activity in Idaho Falls.

These are the major events, the large and tangible
threats that people can react most readily to. But the
smaller things, multiplied many times across this land,
may have equally far-reaching consequences. What is
likely to be the cumulative effect of increasing use of
herbicides and pesticides, proliferation of roads, continual attacks on predators, more and more motorized
toys invading the habitat of wildlife? And how do we
control the real estate developer, who may ultimately
wreak more destruction than all the other threats put
together?

In these ways, Idaho is threatened, yes, but it is not
yet destroyed. The past few years have seen some miraculous events that offer a glimmer of hope. Call it the
spark of an ecological conscience. Or call it panic, perhaps. In any case, a significant number of people have

begun to realize that when the Snake Wilderness is destroyed, there won't be any more. And, surprisingly, this realization is no longer confined to the gasping citizen of Los Angeles or New York. It's here in Idaho, friend. Idaho!

Perhaps the turning point came in December of 1966 when a sheep herder arose at a hearing on the Magruder Corridor. Nervous, unaccustomed to crowds and microphones and hearing rooms, fiddling with his tattered hat and shifting uncomfortably from foot to foot, he allowed as how he'd seen too much country ruined—even helped ruin some himself. It's time to stop, he said. We've got to save some of this wilderness, as much as we can while there's still time.

Perhaps it occurred one year later when eight people decided to keep a dam from being built in Hells Canyon. Organizing the Hells Canyon Preservation Council to inform the public of its options, those conservationists succeeded in what they would have admitted at the time was a lost cause: they have kept the dam out of the Canyon.

Or perhaps it happened more recently, when twenty outraged citizens took on one of the largest mining outfits in the nation, challenging its right to destroy the White Cloud Mountains. That event precipitated one of the most stunning political upsets in the nation, when these same people helped an aroused public elect a strong conservationist to be governor of Idaho.

So we need to ask ourselves whether every state should grow and industrialize like every other. Should we become a homogeneous smear of people and industry and cities from coast to coast, so that each place will be just like every other? Is total californication the goal?

Some of the most important conservation battles in the nation are being fought in the Snake Wilderness. The outcome of these battles could set the tone for future policies on such far-reaching matters as resource use, energy consumption, food production, population growth and industrialization. Idaho's most important role in the future may well be that of showcase to the rest of the nation, an example of how growth and exploitation can be controlled, a demonstration that wilderness is a vital component of our civilization.

# 2. Exploration and Exploitation

To understand the Snake wilderness, one must know a little of its history and of the men who left their marks on it.

The recorded history of the region necessarily begins with the Louisiana Purchase. A few days after signing the document by which France ceded its vast American domain to the United States, President Thomas Jefferson directed Meriwether Lewis, Captain of the First Regiment, U.S. Infantry, to undertake an expedition following the upper Missouri River across unknown territory and traversing the northern Rocky Mountains to the Pacific coast. "The object of your mission," wrote Jefferson," is to explore the Missouri river, & such principal stream of it, as, by its course & communication with the waters of the Pacific Ocean, may offer the most direct & practicable water communication across this continent, for the purposes of commerce." Lewis and his co-leader, Lt. William Clark, carried out these orders faithfully.

Between 1804 and 1806, the Lewis and Clark company explored and traversed the Louisiana Territory in the hopes of finding that elusive Northwest Passage which might link the continent from east to west by a navigable waterway. They found no such thing, of course, but instead crossed some of the most rugged and un-navigable terrain on the continent.

"For the purposes of commerce," however, their journey was reasonably successful because it reinforced the American claim to the Oregon territory, which included virtually all of what are now the states of Oregon, Washington, and Idaho. In addition, the expedition of Lewis and Clark began the "opening up" of the West, an era of exploration and exploitation.

After moving up the Missouri deep into Montana, then southward overland, the Lewis and Clark party first entered the Snake River country and the greater Columbia River drainage by way of Lemhi Pass in the Beaverhead Mountains, now the border between Idaho and Montana. Dropping down into the Lemhi River valley, they followed this river northwest to its confluence with the Salmon, which Clark initially named Lewis's River. (The name Lewis was later transferred to the main stem of the Snake River, which for a number of years was called that by early fur trappers. But the name is now restricted to that tributary of the Snake with headwaters in Shoshone Lake in Yellowstone National Park which joins the Snake at the southern boundary of the Park.) Following the Salmon northward, the party hoped to find a means of navigating it across Idaho, but instead they found its waters wild and dangerous. The steep and rugged Salmon River gorge, now a part of the Idaho Primitive Area, discouraged them from attempting the traverse on foot.

Relying on information from Indians about an easier route, they headed north over what is now Lost Trail Pass, leaving the Snake drainage once again and entering the Bitterroot Valley of Montana. South of present-day Missoula the expedition turned back into the realm of the Snake by crossing over Lolo Pass in the Bitterroot Mountains and arrived at the headwaters of the Lochsa River (the upper end of the Clearwater). From there they followed the Lochsa and the Clearwater, arriving at the Snake River on October 10, 1805, where Lewiston, Idaho, stands today. In the typically unemotional style of his journal, Clark paid tribute to the beauty of this locale by describing the Snake as greenish-blue in color and the Clearwater "as clear as cristial."

The expedition moved on, following the Snake, then the Columbia, to the Pacific coast, where the party wintered before beginning the return journey.

At Lolo Pass on their return trip in 1806, the party split, with Lewis leading a contingent on a northerly, more direct path to the Missouri. Clark's party eventually followed the Yellowstone River north of the Yellowstone Park region. When the two teams regrouped at the confluence of the Yellowstone and Missouri, John Colter, a volunteer with the expedition from the start, received permission to leave in order to join two trappers who were setting out for the unknown reaches of the upper Yellowstone. The adventurous trio departed in August of 1806 on what was to become the next significant journey in Snake River country.

Unfortunately, Colter kept no journals of his travels. He was a bold adventurer, the first of the "mountain men," fur trappers who roamed the Snake River country in search of lucrative beaver pelts. His wanderings took him to the Jackson Hole country, where he doubtless became one of the first white men to view the majestic Teton Range and the upper reaches of the Snake. Colter apparently made camp for the winter of 1807–08 on the Idaho side of the Tetons, not far from the Henry's Fork of the Snake. Then he crossed the northern Tetons to discover some of the incredible features of the Yellowstone region.

The whims of fashion were to dictate the destiny of the Snake River country for the next thirty years. The rage for beaver hats augmented the profit in fur and spurred companies to organize and fund expeditions to exploit what seemed an endless resource of the Rockies. The so-called "golden era" of the mountain men began.

Only five years after Lewis and Clark returned, another expedition—privately funded by John Jacob Astor's American Fur Company—set out from St. Louis. Led by Wilson Price Hunt, the group intended to proceed overland from the Missouri to the mouth of the Columbia, and there establish a trading post to serve as a center of commerce for the exploitation of the Northwest. A companion party left by ship to sail around Cape Horn and meet the Hunt expedition at the Columbia on the Pacific coast. This latter group would retrace Hunt's route on returning to Missouri.

Hunt's path followed that of Lewis and Clark for a short distance up the Missouri. But rumors of hostile Indians led him to abandon that route and head overland through unchartered territory. His course took him to the upper Snake River, through Jackson Hole and across the Tetons, and then over virtually the full length of the Snake River.

Later records revealed that Hunt named many of the

features he encountered, dubbing the upper Snake River
the "Mad River" and calling the Tetons the "Pilot
Knobs." (The name "Tetons" was apparently applied
sometime later by an unknown French trapper, who
called these distinctive peaks "Les Trois Tetons," liter-
ally, the Three Breasts.)

In the early 1820's came the great influx of trappers.
There were several companies active, including the
American Fur Company, the Rocky Mountain Fur Company, and Hudson's Bay Company, as well as many
"free trappers." At the peak of trapping activity, from
1825 to 1835, there were perhaps several hundred men
engaged in it, and their wanderings took them to many
places in the Snake Wilderness: the Salmon River region,
the Lemhi and Lost River Ranges, the Sawtooth and
Hells Canyon country, back and forth across much of
the Yellowstone region, the Absoraka and Wind River
Ranges. They ranged far and wide, into Montana and
Utah, Colorado and New Mexico, Oregon and Washington and northern California. But the hub of activity continued to be the upper Snake and Green River drainages.
Exactly how much territory these men covered may
never be known, but certainly few creeks and streams and
canyons, escaped their searching eyes.

Contrary to the assessments of early historians, few
mountain men truly struck it rich. Although some
amassed fortunes from the fur trade, the vast majority
never realized any riches. In the journals or other accounts a few of them kept of their adventures, they dem-
onstrated surprising sensitivity to the beauty of this wild
country. Hardship and danger were ever-present, of
course, and more than a few lost their lives to Indians or
to the unforgiving harshness of the rivers and mountains.

But many accepted such risks as the price to pay for the privilege of being an adventurer in uncharted territory.

For their exploits, a few mountain men are famous today: Jim Bridger, Joe Meek, Tom Fitzpatrick, the Sublette brothers, Davey Jackson, the legendary Jedediah Smith. And although Nathaniel Wyeth and Captain Bonneville arrived on the scene later than most, they carved their niche in the history of the era. But two men in particular recorded that era with poetry and perception: Osborne Russell and Warren Angus Ferris.

Russell and Ferris were not wide-eyed romantics on a lark, for despite hardship and danger they remained for several years. Ferris was earlier on the scene, arriving on the upper Green River in 1830. As a trapper employed by Astor's American Fur Company, or "The Company" as it was known to the mountain men, Ferris travelled across much of the Snake River country and the northern Rockies. Of his many observations about the country and the trappers' way of life, perhaps his most important and interesting reflection concerns the forces and the motives that attracted the mountain men: "Strange, that people can find so strong and fascinating a charm in this rude and nomadic, and hazardous mode of life, as to estrange themselves from home, country, friends, and all the comforts, elegances, and privileges of civilization; but so it is, the toil, the danger, the loneliness, the deprivation of this condition of being, fraught with all its disadvantages, and replete with peril, is, they think, more than compensated by the lawless freedom, and the stirring excitement, incident to their situation and pursuits. The very danger has its attraction, and the courage and cunning, and skill, and watchfulness made necessary by the difficulties they have to overcome, the privations they are forced to contend with, and the perils against which they must guard, become at once their pride and boast. A strange, wild, terrible, romantic, hard, and exciting life they lead, with alternate plenty and starvation, activity and repose, safety and alarm, and all the other adjuncts that belong to so vagrant a condition in a harsh, barren, untamed, and fearful region of desert, plain, and mountain. Yet so attached to it do they become, that few ever leave it, and they deem themselves, nay are, with all these bars against them, far happier than the in-dwellers of towns and cities, with all the gay and giddy whirl of fashion's mad delusions in their train."

Although he arrived later, Russell stayed longer than Ferris, so enamored was he with this country. In all, Osborne Russell spent nine years as a trapper enjoying the peak years of the fur trade and lasting through the decline. Originally employed by Nathaniel Wyeth, Russell later joined Jim Bridger and finally spent the last few years in the Rockies as a free trapper. His journal, like Ferris's, records with perception something of the essence of the mountain men, as in this entry in 1837 about a winter camp on the Clark's Fork of the Yellowstone River: "We all had snug lodges made of dressed Buffaloe skins in the center of which we built a fire and generally comprised about six men to the lodge. The long winter evenings were passed away by collecting in some of the most spacious lodges and entering into debates arguments or spinning long yarns until midnight in perfect good humour and I for one will cheerfully confess that I have derived no little benefit from the frequent arguments and debates held in what we termed The Rocky Mountain College and I doubt not but some of my comrades who considered themselves Classical Scholars have had some little added to their wisdom in these assemblies however rude they might appear."

There were hardships, of course, and Russell suffered just as many others did. Wounded twice by Indians, he recovered and continued his wanderings. On one occasion, in the bitter cold of late fall in 1837, he and a companion found that their horses and supplies were stolen and had to walk more than a hundred miles to the nearest encampment for help. So adapted, however, were these men to the land and to this way of life, that of one resting place along their journey Russell wrote, "Here we had plenty of wood water meat and dry grass to sleep on, and taking everything into consideration we thought ourselves comfortably situated." He then continued in a philosophic vein: "—comfortably I say for mountaineers not for those who never repose on anything but a bed of down or sit or recline on anything harder than Silken cushions for such would spurn at the idea of a Hunter's talking about comfort and happiness but experience is the best Teacher hunger good Sauce and I really think to be acquainted with misery contributes to the enjoyment of happiness and to know ones self greatly facilitates the Knowledge of Mankind—One thing I often console myself with and that is the earth will lie as hard upon the Monarch as it will on a Hunter and I have no assurance that it will lie upon me at all, my bones may in a few years or perhaps days be bleaching on the plains in these regions like many of my occupation without a friend to turn even a turf upon them after a hungry wolf has finished his feast."

Not many of the mountain men were sensitive or articulate, but, as Bernard DeVoto noted, theirs was a unique life whose freedom and beauty, despite the dan-

gers, held many of them. Such was not the case with
those who came in the 1860's to search for gold.

At another whim of fashion, the market for beaver
pelts declined. But beavers were also becoming scarce, so
successful had the trappers been in their efforts. By 1845
many of them had reluctantly left or were leaving the
Snake country. Some lingered on, yet by the 1850's
much of this land was forgotten and for nearly a decade
it basked once more in relative solitude, traversed occasionally by prospectors on their way to the gold fields of
California. Then gold was discovered in 1860 in the
Clearwater country of Idaho, followed quickly by strikes
in the Salmon River region and the Owyhee Mountains.

The fur trade attracted men who were willing to adapt
to the land. The gold rush brought men who sought to
change it. They were a bawdy, lusty lot, these diggers
who stampeded into Snake country. Driven by greed,
they were largely insensitive to the region's beauty. Had
they had modern technology at their disposal, the devastation would have been immense. They did manage, in
their comparatively crude way, to leave marks: the cen-
tury-old scars here and there of a mine shaft or tailings
pile; the dry, dusty logs of cabins or towns slowly rotting
away. Perhaps their greatest impact, however, was mental
rather than physical. They brought with them the spirit
of exploitation-at-any-cost that became ingrained in the
politics and the people of the region for many years afterward.

The gold, like the fur, did not last, but its impact was
far more critical. Driven by gold fever, men combed the
mountains, valleys, and deserts of the Rockies, as well
as the Sierras, and when a strike was made word spread
rapidly. Within a short time an area would be inun-

dated by a tide of prospectors. Towns would hastily
spring up to be abandoned just as quickly when the gold
played out.

With this great influx of people came that most marked
characteristic of civilization—the political boundary, the
need to distinguish one region from another by arbitrary
lines and names. In 1863 the Territory of Idaho was
established, a vast territory including all of Idaho, Montana, and Wyoming. Within a few years, however, gold
strikes and settlement in the latter two regions resulted
in their being established as separate territories.

On the heels of the gold seekers came the settlers. At
first they simply passed through this country via the
Oregon trail, across the Snake River Plain, or they
headed south from Soda Springs to cross Nevada and on
to California. Eventually some stayed, seeking out first
the lush and verdant mountain valleys. Throughout the
1850's and '60's, when cattle were driven north from
Texas and west from the prairies, ranches were carved
out of the land. Sheep soon arrived. When the tillable
lands were all claimed, new arrivals turned to some of
the more arid regions and attempted to scratch a living
from them. Reclamation and irrigation became a way of
life, beginning first as small water diversions for those
lands close to the Snake or its tributaries and later becoming more massive projects on the big river.

This process of dividing up the land destroyed a culture, one of the saddest and most shameful stories of our
own culture. To the native Americans who had inhabited
this region for tens of thousands of years, the prospectors
and settlers must have been a frightening specter. One
can imagine the natives' frustration when they were trying
to cope with an invasion by people whose values were so

different from their own and whose destructive power was
so great. First, intruders appeared on the scene in search
of beavers, not for a few beavers for their own use, but
for thousands, tens of thousands, that they shipped off
somewhere for some obscure reason. Then the prospectors
came and ravished the earth for a yellow metal of little
practical value. Finally the settlers and ranchers arrived,
selfishly dividing the land, claiming ownership to it when
the People believed that the earth belonged to and sus-
tained all men, not just a few. They destroyed the buffalo,
the Indians' major source of sustenance. And when the
Indians began to defend themselves against this frightening and dangerous horde, they were slaughtered merci-
lessly or rounded up and sent off to reservations.

The change was rapid. Where once great herds of
buffalo and elk had roamed untended, soon there were
cattle that needed to be cared for and nurtured. Where
once the land had been covered with grasses and the wild
camas grew abundant, soon the land was plowed and
strange crops were grown, crops that needed much water
and care. Only now, more than a hundred years too late,
is there a spark of realization that our culture had much
to learn from earlier inhabitants, whose wisdom is best expressed by the words of Smohalla, Nez Percé philosopher:
"My young men shall never work. Men who work cannot
dream; and wisdom comes to us in dreams . . . You ask
me to plow the ground. Shall I take a knife and tear my
mother's bosom? You ask me to dig for stone. Shall I dig
under her skin for her bones? You ask me to cut grass
and make hay and sell it and be rich like white men. But
how dare I cut off my mother's hair?"

Clearly, such madness could not be tolerated in the
tide of an industrial revolution and the westward expan-

sion of a powerful nation. The treaties granting certain lands and rights to the Indians by the United States Government were deliberately broken or ignored by that same government. When new treaties were negotiated, inevitably at a disadvantage to the Indians, they were broken as well.

Such treatment brought about the saddest epoch of American history. As more lands were appropriated, the Indians tried to fight back, only to be defeated and rounded up and shipped to squalid, desolate reservations. Some, like the peaceful Nez Percé, patiently negotiated for more than two decades before deciding that they had to fight for their freedom. This tribe, after seeing the treaties preserving its lands broken by the government and after suffering continual invasions by greedy prospectors and avaricious settlers, was dealt a final blow when the government decided to move it to a reservation to keep it from making trouble. The Nez Percé nation resisted and, led by young Chief Joseph, all of them, men, women, and children, attempted to escape imprisonment by fleeing to Canada in 1877. Taking his people safely across the treacherous Snake River in Hells Canyon, Joseph outfought and outwitted a supposedly superior United States Army across a thousand miles of rugged Rocky Mountain terrain. When, slowed by cold and lack of food, the Nez Percé people were caught just 30 miles short of refuge in the Bearpaw Mountains of northern Montana, they fought desperately, but they lost. And rather than prolong the agony of his people Joseph surrendered with these words: "Tell General Howard I know his heart. What he told me before I have in my heart. I am tired of fighting. Our chiefs are killed. Looking Glass is dead. Too-hul-hul-sote is dead. The old men

are all dead. It is the young men who say yes or no. He
who led on the young men is dead. It is cold and we have
no blankets. The little children are freezing to death. My
people, some of them, have run away to the hills, and
have no blankets, no food; no one knows where they are
—perhaps freezing to death. I want to have time to look
for my children and see how many of them I can find.
Maybe I shall find them among the dead. Hear me, my
chiefs. I am tired; my heart is sick and sad. From where
the sun now stands I will fight no more forever."

Thus, a somewhat blood-tainted Idaho was admitted to the Union in 1890 as the 43rd state. The Indian
"problems" had been largely taken care of. The Snake
country, while not "civilized" like the Eastern United
States, had been roamed and combed and now formalized.
Interestingly enough, settlement in the Snake country
moved largely from west to east, the choicest lands being
in the lower-elevation valleys of the western section. In
fact, the upper reaches of the Snake remained untouched
and unsettled for many years. The Yellowstone and
Teton country was rediscovered by the government expeditions under Ferdinand V. Hayden in the 1870's, expeditions which merely confirmed the stories of the
mountain men thirty years before. And it was that last-
explored reach of the Snake wilderness, Yellowstone,
which was to become the nation's—and the world's—
first national park.

With statehood for Idaho and Wyoming and Oregon,
the Snake country was well on its way toward being
wholly altered and subdued. But two factors have largely
slowed that trend: the establishment and implementation
of a system of public lands, and the generally cold and
arid nature of the region. Harsh climate and lack of

water have slowed development. Large acreage of the Snake River Plain has been put under cultivation, thanks to reclamation schemes, but the vast majority of this land is still desert and rugged mountains. Industrial and population growth have so far been limited to warmer climes or areas more abundant in water.

More effective, perhaps, than climate in keeping the Snake country unspoiled has been the region's public lands program. Because of the vast Public Domain, later to become Bureau of Land Management lands, and because of the establishment of the National Forests and National Park System, more than two-thirds of Idaho is now comprised of publicly owned lands. And despite past and present abuses, these lands can provide insurance for some measure of ecological sanity—for Idaho and the rest of the nation.

# 3. The Last Dam

A dam does violence to a river system. From the moment that the flood gates crash down and the water begins to rise, the life of a living river is choked off.

Over a period of eons of time a river evolves its unique ecology. The flowing water is a habitat to which certain species of aquatic life have adapted, and terrestrial life forms as well have become dependent upon its conditions. Early in its life the river is generally broad and shallow, freshly charged with snowmelt from nearby mountains, and with a water velocity high enough to sweep the river bed clean of all fine sediment and silt, leaving a coarse gravel bed vital as spawning and feeding grounds for certain species of fish.

A river needs to maintain its free-flowing character because the water nourishes itself in life-giving oxygen by aeration as it rushes over rocks and boulders. This tumbling effect also helps maintain the cooler temperatures required by some species. The water quality on many river systems can therefore be considerably impaired by dams. On the Snake-Columbia system there has been a marked increase in dissolved nitrogen in the water, and downstream river temperatures have risen. The nitrogen, trapped under pressure as water goes over dam spillways, expands in the circulatory system of a fish ingesting it, making bubbles and bringing death in a manner similar to that suffered by deep sea divers with the "bends." In addition, the large surface areas of reservoirs ultimately raise river water temperatures by allowing an increase in heating by sunlight. Such alterations endanger some life forms that are extremely sensitive even to small changes in temperature. Increased temperatures at the confluence of the Snake and Columbia have altered the migration pattern of salmon, delaying the runs up the Snake to the Salmon River.

The interface between river and land is also important, for vegetation found along river edges provides both food and shelter for wildlife. Certain species of birds, for example, require shady undergrowth in order to raise their young. Farther away from the river edge the land may be more open and therefore less conducive to certain wildlife forms. This interfacial vegetation has adapted to the river cycle, with its seasonal floods and the gradual drop of water during summer and fall. Such adaptation is possible where fluctuations are natural and gradual, but in reservoirs the drawdown is non-seasonal and often abrupt.

Engineers like to refer to those stagnant reservoirs as "lakes," but there is a vast difference between man-made lakes and natural lakes. Reservoirs must fluctuate radically in level in order to meet power level demands or provide water for irrigation. This fluctuation leaves a sterile, lifeless zone around the perimeter—the so-called bathtub ring effect. If land vegetation attempts to take hold it is flooded out. On the other hand, aquatic vegetation is left high and dry during drawdown.

Dams, of course, flood more than the river interfacial zone. Tens of thousands of acres are often inundated, including canyon bottoms, which in the West are important winter feeding grounds for deer and elk. The recently completed Dworshak Dam on the North Fork of the Clearwater River may be the greatest unsung ecological tragedy of the century, for this project is now flooding approximately 15,000 acres of winter range. Game biologists anticipate losses of up to 40% of the whitetail deer herd, numbering several thousand animals, and about 15% of one of the largest elk herds in the state.

With increasing encroachment of population, with increasing pollution, with proliferating dam schemes on our few remaining unspoiled rivers and streams, hasn't the time come to halt any more construction of dams? Hasn't dam building outlived its usefulness to society, in light of other technological advances? It is now being recognized that flood control may best be accomplished not by building more dams, but by properly zoning the known flood plains and controlling development and logging in critical watersheds—in other words, by planning that takes into account existing natural conditions. Similarly, electricity can be generated by means other than hydro-power, and a long-range, comprehensive study of our society's energy needs can discover better ways to produce *and* conserve it. Furthermore, agricultural production for a stable population does not require more storage dams.

But the cement mixers grind on, despite the increasing numbers of people who question the wisdom of building even one more dam. Just such a project is planned for the heart of Hells Canyon.

Hells Canyon, the deepest river gorge in North America (and, some claim, in the entire world), must also rank as one of the best kept secrets in the nation.

Our country, so obsessed with superlatives, so steeped in the tradition of worshipping whatever is the highest, the longest, the steepest, or the biggest of its kind, has managed somehow to ignore a most extraordinary land feature. Hells Canyon, first explored only a few years after Lewis and Clark, has remained unknown to most Americans. The wildness and relative obscurity of the place have temporarily saved it from the crush of civilization. But, unfortunately, obscurity alone has never saved our wilderness.

In cold, hard statistics, Hells Canyon averages over 5,500 feet in depth. From Dry Diggins Point on the Idaho rim it's a smooth 6,600-foot plunge to the river. And the summit of He Devil Peak, a few miles away, is almost 8,000 feet above the Snake River.

But this place is more than a freak of nature or a record book curiosity. Its wildness and its beauty would remain undiminished even if it were merely the second or tenth or hundredth deepest gorge. Perhaps its most unique characteristic is that it is one of the last free-flowing vestiges of an overdammed, overdeveloped river.

Hells Canyon is a continuum of life and land forms, an entity of wilderness becoming all too rare today. Compressed here within a few miles are all the vegetative life zones of North America, from desert country at river level to alpine tundra in the Seven Devils Mountains. The canyon abounds in both variety and quantity of wildlife. Elk and deer roam the high country, wintering along the river. There are black bears (the grizzly, unfortunately, was exterminated long ago), otter, mink, raccoon, bobcat, and coyote—and the cougar, a rare species in many other places. But the variety isn't limited to terrestrial animals. Peregrine and prairie falcons soar in the heights of the gorge along with golden eagles, ospreys, and sparrow hawks. Closer to the water fly kingfishers and cliff swallows, with Canada geese and other waterfowl nesting along the river in many places.

Aquatic life is truly amazing. Twenty-five species of fish inhabit this section of the Snake, including steelhead, Dolly Varden, chinook salmon, and catfish. It is also one of the last strongholds for the incredible white sturgeon, an ancient though benign relative of the shark. The sturgeon can survive only in swiftly flowing waters, and for millennia has thrived here, where it grows to lengths in excess of ten feet. One of the nation's outstanding wildlife biologists, Dr. Frank Craighead, declares, "It is especially desirable to have an ecological benchmark in the Hells Canyon area because it contains aquatic, terrestrial, and atmospheric habitats that are biologically unique. Nowhere else in the nation are all these species found together in such collective abundance."

But Hells Canyon is also more than a mere catalog of plants and animals. This is a strange and beautiful place where ebony walls rise from the river, giving way to three, even four thousand feet of cliff and grassy hillside, and topped by forested slopes and snow-covered crest. The steep black walls pinch off all but a blue gash of sky, and the heat of the sun seems compressed between these vise-like jaws of rock. There are an awesomeness and grandeur to it all even though, on occasion, it is faintly reminiscent of something out of J. R. R. Tolkein. One can sometimes sense the fears and dangers that prompted early explorers to pronounce it not a singular hell, but many hells. Swift, wild waters; impassable rocky walls; searing 120-degree heat in summer, numbing cold in winter. A canyon of many tortures, many hells. "A river out of hell, the Snake, or a river still in hell," wrote A. B. Guthrie, Jr. "A river making hell for burning souls who couldn't get down to it."

But even the mountain men exaggerated, perhaps, for some of these explorers seemed less concerned with the dangers they faced than with the brooding beauty of this place. "The grandeur and originality of the views presented on every side beggar both the pencil and the pen. Nothing we had ever gazed upon in any other region could for a moment compare in wild majesty and impressive sternness with the series of scenes which here at every turn astonished our senses and filled us with awe and delight," wrote Captain Benjamin L. E. Bonneville, leader of a fur trapping expedition of the early 1830's. Names like Hells Canyon must have been chosen not entirely out of malice, but rather from a grudging admiration for the rugged challenge they represented. And these early adventurers thrived, above all else, on challenge.

The very earliest men on this continent lived in Hells Canyon and left their strange petroglyphs in various dark, hidden places in its depths. Not far from here, on another tributary of the Snake (one which is now inundated by a dam), the oldest remains of human life in North America have been discovered, extending man's knowledge of his species back some 13,000 years. In all likelihood, therefore, Hells Canyon is an untapped treasure of pre-history. Lying near the juncture of two early cultures—the Columbia Plateau and the Great Basin—the canyon may yield important clues to the puzzle of man's arrival and subsequent migration in North America.

And yet, although Hells Canyon is all the things just mentioned, it defies complete description. The cold eye of the camera does little better than words, for it captures only small, finite slices in time of the place's infinite, total flow of life and land. This ecological flow has gone on from time immemorial, and one is tempted to say it will always continue.

But Hells Canyon is threatened by a dam.

Part I of the story about one of the most confusing battles in conservation annals has ended tragically, with the construction of three dams in the upstream reaches of the gorge by Idaho Power Company. With propaganda impugning the patriotism of opponents to their projects, the company laid claim in the 1950's to more than 100 miles of the Snake where today three low hydroelectric dams impound its waters: Oxbow, Brownlee, and Low Hells Canyon dams. Now, the very deepest and wildest part of the canyon is the site chosen for "the last storage project on the Columbia River system." The name of that last dam is High Mountain Sheep. Or Nez Perce. Or perhaps Appaloosa, or Pleasant Valley. It all depends on whom you talk to. And when.

The story opened in 1954 with a proposal to the Federal Power Commission for a two-dam complex consisting of a low regulatory dam at Low Mountain Sheep site, located just above the confluence of the Imnaha River with the Snake, and a 550-foot-high dam at Pleasant Valley, twenty miles farther upstream. Pacific

Northwest Power Company was the applicant, a newly formed amalgamation of four private Northwest power companies: Portland General Electric, Washington Water Power, Montana Power and Light, and Pacific Power and Light. Three years later the Examiner for the Federal Power Commission recommended licensing the project. The following year, however, the full Commission denied the license on the grounds that the full hydroelectric potential of the river would not be realized by this Pleasant Valley-Low Mountain Sheep combination.

Pacific Northwest Power reapplied, this time for a license to build High Mountain Sheep, located just half a mile above the Salmon River-Snake River confluence. An engineer's delight, this 670-foot-high dam (among the world's highest) would create a 58-mile reservoir in the heart of Hells Canyon, flooding twelve miles of the spectacular Imnaha gorge as well.

By 1960 others had their eye on the hydroelectric potential of the canyon. Washington Public Power Supply System (WPPSS), a joint operating agency composed of eighteen public utility districts in the state of Washington, filed application with the FPC for a license to build Nez Perce Dam. This application touched off a flurry of controversy, for Nez Perce, located a mile *below* the Salmon-Snake confluence, would not only finish off the Snake but would flood the lower Salmon River, destroying the anadromous fish runs in this famous "River of No Return." Killing two great rivers for the price of one, Nez Perce promised to become one of the most destructive dams ever built. Washington Public Power later amended its application, proposing to build either High Mountain Sheep or Nez Perce, whichever the FPC felt was best.

It was in this period of time that newly appointed Sec-

retary of Interior Stewart Udall took an active interest
in the Hells Canyon controversy. Arguing that if any
dam was to be built at all it should be built by the
Federal Government, Udall brought the Department of
Interior into the case as an intervenor after the FPC
Examiner once again recommended issuance of license
to Pacific Northwest Power, this time for construction of
High Mountain Sheep Dam. Udall's move has proved to
be the single act to save Hells Canyon so far, for the
subsequent appeals delayed any construction and bought
the time necessary for conservationists to organize an
effort to save the canyon. During the next five years the
legal battle dragged through the lower courts and the
U.S. Court of Appeals (which upheld the FPC decision),
finally reaching the U.S. Supreme Court. In June of 1967
the High Court handed down a landmark decision for
conservation history. Disregarding entirely the question
of who might build the dam, the court directed the
Federal Power Commission to re-examine more carefully
all the arguments, *including the case for no dam at all.*
Delivering the majority opinion, Justice William O.
Douglas stated, "The test is whether the project will be
in the public interest, and that determination can be
made only after an exploration of all issues relevant to
the public interest. These include future power demand
and supply in the area, alternate sources of power, and
the public interest in preserving reaches of wild rivers in
wilderness areas, and the preservation of anadromous
fish for commercial and recreational purposes, and the
protection of wildlife."

In the early years of controversy relatively few conservationists battled the proposals for dams, and these
few had almost given up hope of preventing the construction of High Mountain Sheep. Some even endorsed it,

fearing that the much more destructive Nez Perce might be chosen as an alternative. The American public in general was still unaware of both the proposal and the place, and there was no organized campaign to inform people of the alternatives. Thus the Supreme Court decision offered a chance for conservationists emerging on the Idaho scene, and within a few months an alliance comprised of the Idaho Alpine Club, the Sierra Club, and the Federation of Western Outdoor Clubs filed a petition of intervention with the Federal Power Commission to represent the public interest in the case.

That autumn a handful of Idaho conservationists formed the Hells Canyon Preservation Council for the purpose of rallying public opinion behind the cause of saving the canyon. Like many other citizens' groups then forming across the nation, the Hells Canyon Preservation Council came into existence because neither federal agencies nor elected representatives were responding to growing public concern over environmental problems. Even such regulatory agencies as the Federal Power Commission had become captives of the very industries they were formed to regulate and were consequently no longer serving the public interest in such matters as environmental protection.

Citizen frustration and concern soon gave way to citizen action. As in so many other cases, dam proponents responded to the conservationists by labeling them extremists, or "hysterical preservationists." Interestingly enough, however, the original founders and directors of HCPC were engineers and scientists whose technical expertise and collective man-years of scientific background were probably greater than those of the power companies involved in the project.

The Hells Canyon Preservation Council set about to

win its conservation battle by presenting to the local and the national public information about the resources involved (a wild river and a spectacular canyon) and explaining the available alternatives to a dam. Such conservation battles inevitably begin as a one-sided affair, with the great monetary resources of the exploiters used to sway public opinion in their favor. Company officials on company time and expense frequently travel to towns and cities in the region to talk to local chambers of commerce and civic organizations. Jobs and increased tax revenues are promised. Recreational benefits are touted. Clearly, conservationists operating on a volunteer basis and on limited funds cannot adequately answer these arguments. Furthermore, no federal or state agencies inform the public of the important values to be sacrificed to the project: wildlife and fish; natural wilderness beauty; recreation of a different kind, peaceful and quiet.

In the Hells Canyon case power companies were particularly arrogant, describing the site for their proposed dam as bleak and barren, devoid of any beauty. In its literature, Pacific Northwest Power Company pointed out that "there is the misconception that grows from generalized descriptions of Hells Canyon—the 'deepest' on the North American continent—'steep' wall—'wild' and uncultivated—remote and lonely. It is remote and wild, however, principally because it has little to offer. It is, in no sense, a spectacular gash, like the Grand Canyon of the Colorado." Perhaps the epitome of contempt and arrogance, however, was the statement that "it is Pacific Northwest Power Company's considered judgment that the middle Snake River should be developed and not left as an idle resource."

As the battle wore on, it became increasingly obvious

that the power companies were hardly interested in pursuing alternatives. Caught in the dam-building syndrome, they were reluctant to give up a project that already had cost them several million dollars in engineering design and planning, legal costs, and propaganda efforts. Pacific Northwest Power, like other utilities companies, had become inflexibly bureaucratic, locked into a pattern of selling and over-selling electrons to the public and to industry, committing itself to a pre-planned growth pattern and then fulfilling those self-created electrical needs by the cheapest existing technology, environment be damned (or dammed!). No technological alternatives could be considered in this framework because the power companies spent practically nothing on research for new and cleaner means of generating power. Nor could they assume social responsibility for a campaign, say, to urge less per capita consumption of electrons because of the ever-present profit and loss statement. Caught in their own self-generated, cancerous growth syndrome, the power companies lashed out viciously at the "obstructionists" and the "radical preservationists."

The HCPC began to be effective in an amazingly short time. It was as though the local public had been anxiously awaiting such a group to form. The solid, traditional support for dam building—a way of life in the West—had begun to crumble as more and more sportsmen discovered they had been deceived about the effects of dams on fisheries and wildlife. The salmon and steelhead were threatened, and an increasing number of prime fishing streams had been destroyed by dams. The newly flooded winter range created problems for game animals. Elected representatives, however, were slow in responding to this change in public attitude.

The battle took a new turn when, in the fall of 1968, Senators Len Jordan and Frank Church introduced a bill calling for a ten-year moratorium on dam building in the middle Snake River. (The time period of this moratorium was later reduced to seven years when the bill was re-introduced in the next session of Congress.) This was a crucial first step toward keeping dams out of Hells Canyon, for the Federal Power Commission continued to ignore environmental impact and the spirit of the Supreme Court decision as it leaned toward another issuance of license. The bill followed on the heels of FPC hearings in Lewiston, Idaho, and Portland, Oregon, where the majority of public opinion opposed the dams. Senator Church, apparently coerced into supporting the moratorium by Senator Jordan, felt that time would give conservationists a chance to rally support for saving Hells Canyon.

Senator Jordan, however, an old supporter of pork-barrel reclamation and irrigation dams, made no attempt to hide his reasons for supporting the moratorium concept: delaying the development would undoubtedly force the power companies to pursue other alternatives and their removal from the scene would open the possibility of damming the canyon strictly for reclamation and irrigation schemes. Jordan felt confident that the anadromous fish problem would be resolved one way or another by the time the moratorium ended. Either a way would be found to mitigate the effects of dams on fish, or else they were doomed and would die out. Thus, one of the prime arguments against dams would be removed. His scheme, in collaboration with the Idaho Water Resources Board, was bold: resurrect the old Nez Perce proposal, the difference being that any power generated would

be used to pump the waters of the Salmon and Snake
Rivers back upstream, reservoir by reservoir, in order to
make the southern Idaho desert bloom with more surplus
crops. Conservationists were slow to realize the danger of
the moratorium, but one of Idaho's most astute political
observers noted that the bill seemed counterproductive
to preserving the canyon. More than a month before the
introduction of the moratorium, Bill Hall of the Lewiston
Morning Tribune wrote, "Those who are fighting the
power companies, the public utilities and the federal government to keep hydroelectric dams out of the middle
Snake may be beating a dead horse. As each year passes,
it becomes more difficult to justify corrupting the river
simply to generate more electric energy. There are available alternatives for producing power—especially nuclear
generation which grows more promising every year. If
the battle to save the Snake involved only electric generation, time would be on the side of those who favor a
free-flowing stream. . . . In short, time may be on the
side of those who would dam the middle Snake for reclamation purposes, even if it is not on the side of those
who would build additional and almost obsolete hydroelectric dams." A new threat to Hells Canyon had appeared.

The Hells Canyon Preservation Council had been
working on its own proposal to protect Hells Canyon and
the middle Snake River. In consultation with fish and
wildlife experts, local and national conservation groups,
and people with intimate knowledge of the Hells Canyon
country, the Council carefully considered several legislative packages. To preserve the Snake as a Wild and
Scenic River was ruled out, for such classification, as

stipulated by the Wild and Scenic Rivers Act, would
allow protection of only a quarter-mile strip on either
side of the river, leaving the vast wilderness in the high
country unprotected. Creating a national park was also
eliminated because of the strongly negative attitude toward parks of most sportsmen, whose support was needed
for a broad-based proposal. Thus the concept of a Hells
Canyon-Snake National River emerged, a unique piece
of legislation which would provide the necessary protection, particularly Wilderness Area designation for the
great unspoiled areas of the canyon, the lovely forested
plateau on the Oregon side, and the rugged Seven Devils
Mountains in Idaho. In total, the Hells Canyon-Snake
National River would embrace some 720,000 acres,
400,000 acres of which would be protected as wilderness. This proposal received strong support from virtually
all conservation and sportsmen's organizations, but conservationists ran into difficulties in finding a sponsor for
the bill.

Senator Church refused to introduce the bill in the
Senate, citing his pledge of support to Senator Jordan on
the moratorium bill as the reason. Oregon Senator Mark
Hatfield also refused, which was not surprising in light
of his general anti-conservation attitude. In the fall of
1969 conservationists approached Oregon's other Senator, Bob Packwood, a young, dynamic freshman senator
who enthusiastically agreed to sponsor the bill. He introduced it in the Senate the next January.

In the House of Representatives, it was impossible to
find a congressman from Oregon or Idaho willing to
sponsor the legislation. Idaho Congressman James Mc-
Clure, in whose district Hells Canyon is located, was
quite opposed to preserving it, and his voting record

indicated strong alignment with exploitative interests like logging, mining, and dam proponents. McClure, in fact, would not support even the moratorium, apparently because he was anxious to see the dams built quickly. On occasion, in the privacy of his office, he was openly antagonistic and abusive to constituents who favored preserving the canyon. Idaho's other congressman, newly elected Orval Hansen, weakly aligned himself with the Church-Jordan moratorium position and quickly refused to consider any other action. Idaho conservationists felt betrayed because they had supported Hansen in his bid for the congressional seat. Representative Al Ullman, whose Oregon district embraces Hells Canyon, was also strongly anti-conservation. After introduction of the National River bill by Pennsylvania Representative John Saylor, the House of Representatives' outstanding conservationist and the only sympathetic congressman conservationists could find, Ullman retaliated with a bill designed to confuse the issue in the public eye. His measure, written for him by the U.S. Forest Service, called for the establishment of a National Recreation Area in Hells Canyon, a weak proposal which would allow dams to be built and other destructive activities, like logging, to be carried on. Both McClure and Ullman sit on the House Interior and Insular Affairs Committee, through which the National River bill must pass. Thus, conservationists are confronted with the grim reality that Hells Canyon will probably not be protected while McClure, Ullman, and probably Hansen, remain in office.

In February of 1970 the Senate Subcommittee on Water and Power held a hearing on the Church-Jordan moratorium bill. More than half of the witnesses and individual letters supported the National River bill over the moratorium, with much additional testimony implicitly endorsing it by stating strong opposition to any dams. After the hearing Senator Church admitted privately that, though his moratorium bill would pass the Senate easily, it had little chance of moving in the House. Should it die there, he promised, he would pursue some other course of action to help save Hells Canyon. His statement led conservationists to believe that he would support the Hells Canyon-Snake National River bill.

As predicted, the moratorium passed the Senate in 1970, but the House failed to take any action. Rather than keep his promise to conservationists, however, Senator Church once again joined in re-introducing the moratorium in early 1971. This time Oregon Senator Mark Hatfield joined in the sponsorship.

Conservationists continue to argue that a moratorium isn't needed. The middle Snake River has been studied for twenty years or more, and enough is known about it *now* to declare it worthy of protection. Because the moratorium is designed, in the words of the three senators, to "keep the options open," it is certain that passage of this bill will forestall any action on the National River proposal or any other means of permanent protection for seven years. In addition, while the moratorium would forestall dam-building, it would not prevent other destructive activities from going on. Private parcels of land, for example, the remnants of early homesteads which are scattered along the river, are now being sought by large land developers. In addition, mining, logging, and road-building would continue unabated under the moratorium. And reclamation forces, still politically powerful in Idaho, are rallying for an assault on Hells Canyon with the encouragement of Senator Jordan. For these reasons, conservationists consider the moratorium a sellout to reclamationists and developers.

In February 1971 the Federal Power Commission Examiner, William R. Levy, after four years of additional deliberation and collection of evidence, once again recommended issuance of a construction license to the combine comprised of Pacific Northwest Power and Washington Public Power Supply System. This time, however, the license authorized the Pleasant Valley-Low Mountain Sheep Dam combination, the original proposal of 1954. Levy's only concession to environmental considerations was to add the recommendation that construction be deferred for five years to allow the preservation issue to be settled. The full Federal Power Commission will probably uphold his decision, though it may be a year or two before they do so. Despite the de facto moratorium recommended by the FPC Examiner, conservationists plan to appeal the licensing decision and will carry the appeal to the Supreme Court again if necessary. This legal process promises to tie up the dam proposal for several more years.

In early 1971 the Church-Jordan-Hatfield moratorium bill was voted out of the full Senate Interior and Insular Affairs Committee, even though support for it at the hearing was lukewarm. Just before a floor vote in the full Senate in June, Senator Packwood announced that he would offer a floor amendment which would substitute his Hells Canyon-Snake National River bill, S.717, for the moratorium. Senator Packwood, working hard to save the Snake, managed to find an additional 26 senators willing to co-sponsor his amendment. It was a bold move, unconventional, perhaps, but cheered by conservationists because it would focus attention on the plight of Hells

Canyon and probably force hearings to be scheduled on
the National River bill (Packwood's plea for hearings on
his bill had thus far fallen on deaf ears).

At this point Senator Church, who appeared finally to
recognize the popularity of the save-Hells Canyon-move-
ment in Idaho, could have played a passive role, letting
Senator Jordan lead the fight to scuttle the Packwood
Amendment. Instead, he too fought actively against it,
almost vindictively, co-signing with Senators Hatfield and
Jordan a "Dear Colleague" letter sent to all other members of the Senate. This letter reads like something
straight out of the reclamation era of the 1930's and
1940's. Stating that "The importance of future water
requirements of Idaho and Oregon cannot be overesti-
mated" and ". . . we believe that the semi-arid states
involved deserve the opportunity to keep their options
open until Federally assisted water resources planning
can be completed," the letter implies endorsement of
reclamation schemes for the middle Snake River. It also
suggests that Hells Canyon should not be "locked up"
by such measures as designating it a National River.

That Senator Church signed such a letter shocked
conservationists. For in 1965 this same Frank Church
in a discussion of the inclusion of the Salmon and Clearwater Rivers in the National Wild and Scenic Rivers bill
before a hearing in Lewiston, Idaho, had declared, "Nor
am I impressed with the argument that further study is
needed before any judgment can be reached for or
against the inclusion of the designated parts of the Salmon and Clearwater Rivers in the national wild rivers
system. What additional information, not now available,
will more delay furnish? What facts are now lacking?
*For fifty years we have been accumulating exhaustive*

*data on the whole Columbia-Snake River drainage. We
have the complete record of the river flows, of the salmon
runs, the flood cycles, and the navigational irrigational
and hydroelectric potential of every river and tributary
in the Northwest.*

*"We have all the necessary information at hand. The
issue should not be dodged on the flimsy pretext that
more facts are needed."* (emphasis added)

Senator Packwood withdrew his amendment before
the floor vote when a promise was given of hearings on
S.717. The moratorium subsequently passed the Senate
to await House action.

When hearings were held on Senator Packwood's National River bill, in September of 1971, much of the bitterness generated by the moratorium fight earlier in the
year lingered on. The Subcommittee on Parks and Recreation, chaired by Senator Allan Bible, conducted the
hearings. Senators Church and Hatfield were members of
that Subcommittee. Senator Jordan, in his capacity of
member of the full Interior and Insular Affairs Committee, was given permission to sit in. Senator Packwood,
who was not a member of the Interior Committee, had
to obtain special permission to sit on this subcommittee.

Senator Packwood, the leadoff witness, was grilled unmercifully for nearly three hours. The major point of
contention was the almost hysterical fear that the National River bill would pre-empt water used for *upstream*
irrigation projects. Repeatedly, Senator Packwood pointed
out that his bill studiously avoided any wording which
would affect upstream usage. But his words fell on deaf
ears, and it soon became apparent that the question of
water pre-emption was merely an excuse for the reclamation and irrigation proponents to oppose this bill.

The hearing was a disaster for supporters of the Hells Canyon-Snake National River bill. For two days a parade of exploitative interests went before the committee to oppose the bill, including the director of the Idaho Water Resources Board, the present commissioner of the Bureau of Reclamation, the director of the National Forest Products Association, a vice president of Boise Cascade lumber company, the general manager of the Northwest Public Power Association, the Washington representative of the Georgia-Pacific lumber company, the executive director of the Idaho Reclamation Association, the chairman of the Idaho Public Land Resources Council (a front group for exploitative industries), the president of the Washington State Labor Council, the director of Pacific Northwest Power Company, the executive director of Washington State Public Utility Districts Association, the general manager of American Public Power Association, the executive secretary of Southern Idaho Forestry Association, the executive director of National Water Resources Association. And others. Chambers of Commerce, ranchers, farmers, multiple-use organizations fronting for exploitative interests—all were well organized and financed. Apparently Senator Jordan had spent much time frightening his reclamation friends with the spectre of *preserving* Hells Canyon (and thus preventing realization of grandiose pork-barrel schemes for irrigating more desert land). The old bogey-man—fear of someone "stealing" Idaho water—was raised again and again.

Even to the casual observer the hearing was run with the deck stacked against conservationists. One tactic was to give reclamation proponents more time on the witness stand. The committee chairman had set a strict five-minute time limit for presentation of statements. No time limit was set, however, for question and answer. Thus many long questions were asked of opponents to the National River bill in order to allow them more time to elaborate on their statements. Conservationists, however, who had no friends on the committee, were not asked questions which would allow elaboration of their point of view. The director of the Idaho Water Resources Board spent over an hour at the witness table expounding on the need for dams, whereas the northwest representative of the Sierra Club was silenced after five minutes. Senator Packwood attempted to help, but he was frequently cut off by the chairman. Senator Jordan, on the other hand (who was also a "guest" on this committee), was allowed unlimited time in his ponderous questioning and his sometimes vitriolic attacks.

Some of the hearing witnesses were surprising and perhaps a little pitiful. Conrad Wirth, the former director of the National Park Service, who opposed the bill, made a sales pitch for the recreation benefits of the dams in rambling, almost incoherent testimony. At one point he denied any connection with the power companies and a few moments later admitted to Senator Packwood that he was working for Pacific Northwest Power Company and Washington Public Power Supply System.

At times the hearing took on a bizarre aspect, as when the president of the Southwest Idaho Water Development Association angrily demanded that outsiders keep their hands off "our" water and "our" lands, referring to the lands and the resources belonging to the entire nation. And the executive director of the Idaho Reclamation Association asserted that "you can flirt with my wife, but don't touch my water."

Even Floyd Dominy, the former commissioner of the

Bureau of Reclamation, suggested that if the National
River bill should pass, "then we should, at the same time,
ask the President to invoke the provisions of the Act of
September 30, 1950—popularly known as the Federal
Disaster Act." Dominy, still the outspoken hero of the
die-hard dam builders, ripped into conservationists. "I
think . . . that many people are being misled by well-
organized campaigns from a few people in terms of the
real needs in the United States of America." But his main
theme was the one he had espoused for many years: un-
controlled, wild, undeveloped rivers are a waste and
man's technology can improve upon nature. He ridiculed
the idea that a dam would harm Hells Canyon. "The
vast Snake River Canyon will still be there relatively un-
changed from its natural splendor. And the developed
river as far as a majority of our citizens are concerned
would be an improvement over nature because it would
be contributing valued economic benefits, and would
make the general scenic values of the area vastly more
accessible for the use and enjoyment of man."

The threat of hydroelectric dams for Hells Canyon
has nearly passed. Now it's reclamation dams. The transition from one to the other has been very subtle; the
threat is just as real.

Reclamation. What does it mean? To *re-claim* means
to rescue or bring back, to obtain something useful from
something wasteful. The general theory goes like this:
water makes things grow. Deserts have no water. Therefore, if you bring water to a desert you can grow all
kinds of things. Like money.

The fine points are more subtle. First, several businessmen form a corporation—a farming corporation.
Then, under the Desert Land Entry Act (something little

known to people today, and roughly akin to the Home-
stead Act), they file claims on public lands (meaning
yours and mine) for purposes of obtaining title to this
land for private uses—to farm. But there's no water.
Next, the businessmen set about promoting reclamation
projects, such as a dam in Hells Canyon, funded by
public money (again, yours and mine). Can't let all that
water leak out of Idaho unused! This part is easy, given
the eager aid of state agencies like the Idaho Water Resources Board and federal agencies like the Bureau of
Reclamation and some elected representatives, all supported by . . . Right! Public money.

When the project is completed, the businessmen,
through their farming corporation, can make an immense
profit growing crops on land they paid nothing for, with
water they got practically free. In a few years, having
established bona fide farms, producing surplus crops,
they may soon begin collecting massive farm subsidies
for *not* growing these crops. And when they get bored
making money that way, they can ultimately subdivide
the land, selling off half-acre "rancheros" for a few
thousand dollars each.

Absurd? Yes. Unreal? No. Such projects are already
under way in the desert of southwest Idaho. It's called,
appropriately enough, the Southwest Idaho Water Development Project. Initially it will tap the water from the
Snake River nearby, but undoubtedly the project will
serve as a forerunner to more grandiose plans involving
one or more dams in Hells Canyon. Is it needed? An increasing number of concerned citizens are beginning to
wonder. Among them are Drs. Chapman, Falter, and
Rabe, ecologists at the University of Idaho, who under-
took a study for the Department of the Army on the

project. Their report, entitled Ecological Evaluation of
the Mountain Home Division, Southwest Idaho Water
Development Project, begins with a blunt discussion of
the futility of the project in terms of its ability to meet
the need for increased food production to serve an exploding population. Here are their words:

> We, as ecologists, face a dilemma. To evangeli-
> cally embrace our ecological and social philosophy
> whole-heartedly, we would fight every environ-
> mental insult and constantly crusade for population
> control. We would oppose technological and agri-
> cultural changes that lull man as he drifts toward
> apocalypse. In other words we would follow the
> dictates of our ecological conscience.
>
> On the other hand, as humanists we feel obli-
> gated to improve human welfare in the short run.
> This includes providing food for our own hungry and
> those in undeveloped nations. If we bring the present
> world population to our caloric intake (about 2,600
> K cal/day) world food production must increase
> several-fold (Hulett, 1970).
>
> We do not look upon new land entry as a panacea
> for inadequate present food production. A total of
> 490,000 acres of new irrigable land in the four
> divisions of the Southwest Idaho Water Develop-
> ment Project could produce the following annual
> equivalents: 35,000,000 bushels of wheat, 100,-
> 000,000 pounds of potatoes, or 750,000 tons of hay
> or 7,500,000 pounds of beef. Deduct 20% from
> each figure to compensate for nonproductive land
> uses . . . access roads, power transmission lines,
> irrigation canals and feeders, building sites, and

farm buildings. *The resulting agricultural production would supply food needs for a maximum of
100,000 people.* With a national population growth
rate of 3 million people per year, *these new lands
would support less than 12 days' worth of our additions to this country's population.* (emphasis added)

We see food production as a problem in subop-
timization. Resource economists and other govern-
mental advisors must address themselves to these
questions: "What is the best way to optimize agricultural output with limited funds? Shall we expand cultivated acreage, irrigate more on existing
acreage, or use other technical advances and minimize inefficiency to expand production on existing
acreage?" In other words, does the Mountain Home
reclamation project offer the most food return for
the dollars invested, and if not, what other proposal
would do so?

Planners of a national course of action to supply
future resource needs need not rush headlong into
resource development in the interest of increasing
food and raw materials development to "solve" current and impending problems of limited vital needs.
By doing so, we may only push ourselves further out
on the limb in the race to satisfy the ever-expanding
needs of our ever-expanding population. The time
of reckoning is put off, not abolished.

# 4. "Certainly we're going to make a big hole."

"We'll be removing tons of ore and rock, but it's our intention to do it with a minimum of disruption. What we can do is to re-establish the ecological system in the area to as high a value as it is now. We're sure we can do that. The landscape won't look the same as it does now. Maybe it might even be a little better."

Supervisor of Northwest Exploration
American Smelting and Refining Company

In the settling of Idaho, civilization flowed quietly around the White Cloud Mountains. Actually, that term "civilization" may be misleading, for even today the region is sparsely populated. West of this range is the lovely valley of Stanley Basin, a lush green carpet rimmed on its western perimeter by the spectacular Sawtooth Mountains. Hemmed in by mountains on all sides, this valley is an area of productive ranch lands. The diminutive town of

Stanley (population 35) is located here. Many of its buildings are original log cabins of an era passed.

North of here the town of Challis grew up in the aftermath of nearby mining. The mines played out, as all mines must, but the town remained when ranching and logging became the economic base. Similarly, to the south, Ketchum first developed as a mining town and later struck real pay dirt with a ski development called Sun Valley.

Roads and highways came: over Galena Summit, into and out of Stanley Basin, following the twisting Salmon River north; down through the Big Lost River Valley, with a few dusty spurs climbing off into dry foothills; over Trail Creek Pass, the informal separation between the Boulder and Pioneer Mountains; and then along the East Fork of the Salmon, touching the few isolated ranches while offering tantalizing views of distant Castle Peak, landmark of the remote White Clouds.

But even with the towns, the roads and highways, and the gradual influx of people, the heart of the White Clouds remained inviolate, though occasional attempts were made to penetrate it. True, on Big Boulder Creek the Livingston Mine scratched lead and silver out of the earth, supported a handful of people for a few years, and then left behind several centuries' worth of scars when it folded. Still, the area remained largely wilderness, more than 150,000 acres of gleaming peaks and cool alpine lakes. If any place has clearly needed special protection, this one has. The United States Forest Service, however, never saw fit to classify it as a Wilderness or Primitive Area to give it that added measure of defense against encroachment. The agency claimed that in recent years an informal wilderness management policy had been adopted, though simultaneously it actively encouraged motorized intrusion of the fragile high country by trail bikes. But perhaps its obscurity gave the area its best protection: in a state so amply endowed with wild mountain country, the White Clouds were relatively unknown. Transported physically to Ohio or New Jersey, these mountains would have become a national park long ago, venerated and celebrated on a wide scale. Here, they were run-of-the-mill spectacular in a state of spectacular plenty.

Other prospectors wandered through, dug some holes and tunnels, and then moved on. Over the years, all the mountains in this region, the White Clouds, the Pioneers, the Boulders, and the Sawtooths, had been crossed and re-crossed in the search for minerals, the hope of instant riches. But the voracious appetite of modern industry demanded more than the small, scattered pockets of surface minerals could satisfy. Gradually, the high grade stuff was gone, and along with it the myth of the one-man bonanza. What minerals remain are very deep, very dilute, or very remote. It takes big money and big holes to mine today.

Trouble began in 1968 with a rumor, which was then confirmed in a phone call from Ernie Day of Boise: something's going on in the White Clouds. Mineral discovery. No small-time prospectors, but apparently something big. Corporate money. Helicopters and expensive drilling rigs all around Castle Peak. *Have you seen it?* No, but others have first hand. It's bad. *How long has it been going on?* Several months—started even before the snow was out. *But an operation that big would surely catch the eye of the Forest Service—any word from them?* None. *Surely the Forest Service wouldn't keep it a secret, would they?* Would they? *What do we do?* Check it out.

By September official press releases and articles had confirmed the worst fears. A huge open pit mine would be dug near the base of Castle Peak. Several hundred acres of claims had been filed by American Smelting and Refining Company (ASARCO), one of the largest mining companies in the world, and several hundred adjacent acres were claimed by Taylor Mining of Denver. ASARCO, it seems, had made a major find of molybdenum, a hard, silver-white metal useful mainly as an alloying agent in hardening steel. The mineral molybdenite has been located at reported depths of 400 to 600 feet in a basin just over the northeast flank of 11,820-foot Castle Peak, and scattered over a large enough area to warrant stripping tons of overburden rock to get at it. Though both deep and dilute (the ore averaged only 0.2% molybdenum), there was enough metal to sustain a mining operation for twenty to thirty years.

ASARCO's plans would include a huge tailings pond which would cover five to six miles of Little Boulder Creek with hundreds of feet of waste; a processing mill; an access road to be blasted into the high country; power lines, and all the other accoutrements of a big mining venture. Summed up, these plans spelled instant devastation for the White Clouds wilderness.

In retrospect, one doubts that the company was aware of the subtle change in sentiment growing in Idaho during the past several years. If it had, it might have considered handling things differently. As it was, initial press releases gave glowing accounts of the great discovery, glorifying the company's plans for the massive open pit and extolling the mine's great economic assets to the state and county: payrolls and tax rolls would rise, and income would accrue from the thousands of tourists who would flock to see this man-made hole. The photographs in those releases showed proud men clustered around their drill rigs, like true conquerers of the wilderness. (Such irony aside, it was doubtless an exciting discovery.) In subsequent interviews, the geologists and drillers made their jobs seem idyllic as they described the beauties of living in the heart of this unspoiled alpine country. Their work, of course, would mean its ultimate destruction.

Only five years earlier, news about a mine would have barely caused a ripple. But change had been fermenting. A new breed had been arriving during the past decade, many of whom has seen environmental depredations elsewhere, and, in moving here, had come to love this unspoiled country for what it was, not for its selling price.

There was growing evidence of this shift in attitudes. Each hearing on environmental matters drew more and more people willing to stand up in defense of wilderness and wild rivers. Fledgling organizations such as the Hells Canyon Preservation Council, formed in 1967, were receiving increasing, enthusiastic support. The Hells Canyon organization actually played an important role in the early White Cloud fight. In just a year's time, that group rallied an amazing amount of local and national support. People began to feel that it might be possible to succeed, just as those in Hells Canyon had succeeded so far in staving off the dam threat.

It was within this framework that news of the White Cloud mining venture broke. Whether ASARCO anticipated it or not, reaction to its proposal was swift and deafening. Major papers in the state denounced the imminent rape of the White Clouds, citing it as one more tragic example of the need for reform in the nation's antiquated mining laws.

The venture became the state's biggest news story within a few months. During the fall of 1968, day after day, condemnation of the mining scheme by conservationists rated the front page. And letters to newspaper editors monopolized editorial pages.

Battle lines were quickly drawn. Governor Don Samuelson leaped to the miners' defense, as did the citizens of nearby Challis and some chambers of commerce in the region. Their arguments were familiar: growth, progress, money, free enterprise. Even God and patriotism found their way into some statements. "The good Lord never intended us to lock up our resources" became one of the more famous remarks of the Governor. But despite vociferous defense of the miners by the Governor and officials of his administration, the public seemed outraged by the imminent destruction of the White Clouds.

Public outcry was hardly enough, however. A focal point was needed, an organization was required to turn public sentiment into action. Thus the Greater Sawtooth Preservation Council came into existence.

Thirty-five people met in a living room in Idaho Falls for the first strategy session of the new organization. Things looked grim. With an initial membership of less than fifty and an operating budget of $125, the Council seemed pitifully ill-equipped to take on a corporate giant. Under the 1872 mining laws the company had a legal right to do as it wished, and, since claims had been properly filed, there seemed to be no way to stop the operation by litigation. Only two actions appeared to offer any im-

mediate hope for stalling it. The first concerned the
validation process for the claims. In order for a claim to
be valid (and thus eventually be patented, or pass from
public to private ownership), proof of an actually minable
ore deposit must be established. In the past, this process
had been a mere formality for the mining companies.
Legally, a deposit is considered economically feasible to
mine, and thus subject to validation, if a "prudent man,"
investing his own time and money to mine, process, and
market the mineral, could expect a reasonable return
for his efforts. Until recent years, not many claims validated on this ground had been challenged. And in the
case of the ASARCO claims, few people doubted that
sufficient molybdenum was there to mine economically.
Still, if each of the hundreds of claims had to be validated
separately, the bureaucratic process might take months,
thereby giving conservationists a little breathing space.

The other hope lay in the question of access. With
the claims area lying some eight miles from the nearest
road, ASARCO had officially filed for a special use permit
from the Forest Service to construct a road up the Little
Boulder Creek drainage, starting from the East Fork of
the Salmon River. Again, the statutes seemed vague, offering only "reasonable" ingress and egress to claims across
public lands. Since the statutes did not specify that access
had to be by road, the Forest Service might be talked into
considering other means of access, such as tramways
(someone also suggested a tunnel). And the deliberative
process before a road construction permit would be issued
could also buy time. As long as there was no road, there
would be no mine. Even with all its money, ASARCO
could not afford to haul ore by helicopter.

Immediate action of some kind was necessary. For the

winter the miners had halted their exploratory drilling operations, but with the coming of spring, activity would be resumed. John Merriam, the newly elected president of the Greater Sawtooth Preservation Council, summed up the crisis: "Unless we act soon, the countdown on the White Clouds is T minus six months for bulldozers."

Discussion up to this time had concerned only stopgap measures. If the Council succeeded in stalling the project, its next step was to have long-range plans for permanently protecting the White Clouds and surrounding country. Legislation had to be considered carefully, for there was no legal way to take away valid claims. Even a miraculous repeal of the mining laws could not be made retroactive in order to negate ASARCO's rights. In considering legislation, then, two things were vital: 1) all surrounding unclaimed lands must be withdrawn from further claim filing or mineral entry, and 2) some form of special land management classification should be assigned to the whole area and the managing agency given the power and authority to regulate and control access to the mine, and to control the use of surrounding lands as well. If standards were set high enough and controls were stringent enough, the deposit might become uneconomical to mine. Ten miles of road through rugged country could become very expensive to build and maintain if extremely high standards of construction and maintenance were set in order to protect the environment. Moreover, since tailings ponds and processing mills require special use permits by a managing agency before they can be constructed, stringent environmental standards could add greatly to their cost.

There was one additional, important possibility to consider. If legislation making the area a national park should pass *before* the claims were validated and patented, it could have an important effect on *whether* the claims could ever be patented. For it could then be argued that no "prudent man" would ever mine in a national park because restrictive regulations would make it too expensive and because no additional land would be made available for processing and waste dumping. The whole thing would be a massive squeeze play, a Catch-22, to force the miners out.

During the first few months of the controversy, the U. S. Forest Service came under fire for its apparent willingness to sacrifice the White Clouds without a fight. Because the claims were filed on National Forest lands, the Service had jurisdiction to act on the question of claim validation and access. Undoubtedly, its initial timid actions were dictated by fear of incurring the wrath of the politically powerful mining industry. With time, however, it became apparent that conservationists were rallying public opinion behind them. As a result, in the spring of 1969 the Forest Service announced that it would hold public hearings ostensibly to gather information about the question of an access road permit for the miners.

The Forest Service was careful to state in its announcements that it was legally bound to allow some means of access to the claims and that hearings would only elicit ideas on how best to minimize environmental impact of the access. But regardless of the announced reasons, these hearings became the sounding board that conservationists had been hoping for—a chance for the public to say what it really thought about the prospect of destroying the White Clouds.

Several hundred people attended the hearings in Boise and Idaho Falls, with testimony running three to one and seven to one, respectively, against the mine. Even among those present who did not testify, the sentiment was clearly anti-mining. A third hearing at Challis ran overwhelmingly in support of the mining plan, with the predominance of testimony citing economic benefits. Many citizens of the Challis area expressed anger over "outsiders" trying to dictate what should or should not be done with "their" lands. Privately some residents opposed the mine, but they were reluctant to speak out, perhaps fearing social ostracism. Emotions reached the boiling point. The mining industry's representatives had spent much time in the Challis community cultivating support by promising great riches. Now that this wealth was being threatened by a bunch of "preservationists," there was anger.

The hearings were not the first face-to-face encounter in the state between conservationists and the mining industry, but they did mark the beginning of a large-scale public debate, not only on the White Clouds, but also on resource matters of a broader scope, arguments and philosophy to which a large segment of the Idaho public had never been exposed before. The industry declared that mining and mineral exploration are the very cornerstone of the free enterprise system. The freedom to exploit and develop such resources has made America the great power it is today, the miners claimed, and molybdenum is one of the strategic materials needed to maintain industrial might. Mineral deposits are where you happen to find them, they argued, and industry should be free, within reason, to develop these deposits wherever they occur.

And because such mining activity represents a relatively
small percentage of the total public land area, what's left
can be preserved for ecological reasons.

Conservationists were quick to point out that, according to U. S. Bureau of Mines statistics, molybdenum is
not in short supply. In known reserves, not counting the
White Cloud deposit, there is an estimated one hundred
years' supply of the metal in this country. Furthermore,
since almost a third of this country's production of the
metal is exported, it seemed almost profane to sacrifice
magnificent wilderness for the sake of corporate expansion
into foreign markets. As to the cornerstone-of-industry
theory, conservationists argued that we cannot continue
to consume incredible quantities of resources for the
manufacture of throwaway, non-returnable products. Recycling of everything from autos to beer cans must be
made economically feasible and highly efficient to allevi-
ate the need for further rape of the land. Others indicated that although the relative percentage of land utilized
for mining is small, the impact extends far beyond the
confines of pit or tunnel to surrounding lands and waters.
They noted that open pit or strip mining does the most
violence to land, destroying all living things on the surface and creating unhealing scars visible from long dis-
tances. Mining also means surface disruption by roads,
power lines draped across the land to supply energy, and
air and water pollution from mills and smelters.
ASARCO's record on the last score is particularly bad,
with pollution controversies and lawsuits concerning seri-
ous pollution problems pending against the company in
Texas, Arizona, California, Montana, and Washington.
In Tacoma, for example, the ASARCO smelter dispenses
a blessing of twenty-two tons per hour of sulfur dioxide

into the city's atmosphere. Claiming that the danger of
sulfur dioxide to human health has been "grossly exaggerated," ASARCO has attempted economic extortion by
threatening to shut down the plant if forced to comply
with air pollution standards.

At the Forest Service hearings ASARCO representatives revealed more specifically what the mining operation would entail. Based on their current estimates of size
and location of the ore, a 7,000-foot-long pit would be
dug to a depth of between 300 and 400 feet and a width
of about 700 feet. Planned operation would be at the
processing rate of forty million pounds of ore per day for
an estimated twenty years. With a content of only 0.2%
molybdenum, 99.8% of the ore removed would be waste.
In order to handle that waste material, the company proposed a 400-foot-high dam on Little Boulder Creek to
create a tailings pond, or a series of ponds, several miles
long. During the life expectancy of the mine, some *145
million tons* of waste material would be deposited there.

In answer to expressions of concern over polluting the
Salmon River drainage, ASARCO promised that the
White Cloud operation would be different from most
others. Every effort would be made to minimize the environmental impact, it said, and when the operation was
completed in twenty or thirty years, the pit would be
filled with water to create a lake of great recreational
value. Restoration of the land would be the company's by-
word, and to prove good faith it had even hired an
ecology consultant.

Either with or without the blessings of hired experts,
industry's attempts at so-called restoration of strip mined
lands has been far less effective than the public relations
campaigns would indicate. In fact, restoration in the strict

definition of the word is impossible; the land can not be returned to its former state in any ecological (or esthetic) sense after mining. Soil, a living medium that takes millennia to create, can not be manufactured. What the mining companies have attempted, and what ASARCO promised, is reclamation, not restoration. Attempts have been made, with varying degrees of success, to reclaim mined-over lands by planting hardy species of trees and grasses, but the diverse ecosystem remains seriously impaired. It takes time—several thousand years of it—for nature to restore such damaged land.

When the hearings were concluded, the Forest Service announced that it would deliberate on the matter and conduct a study of various access alternatives. In the meantime, no permit would be issued—a temporary victory for the conservation forces.

In the ensuing months a surrealistic battle began, one that would continue unabated well into the next year. A steady stream of press releases issued from the Governor's office was condemning those who were opposing or delaying the mine. At a Western Governors' Conference in Seattle, Samuelson publicly chastised Forest Service Chief Ed Cliff for even allowing public hearings on the matter and blamed the agency for stirring up the public. "If you had just gone ahead and issued the permit," Samuelson told Cliff face to face, "there would have been no controversy."

Later, Samuelson accused the Forest Service of deceit. "The administration of the Forest Service in this region stinks to high heaven," he proclaimed, adding that the agency was deceiving the public with claims that the mine would be located in the heart of the White Cloud Mountains. Incredibly, the governor claimed that the proposed location was *not* in the White Clouds at all, adding that the area affected was merely dry, barren sagebrush lands. If it had not become clear by this time, the relationship between the governor and the mining industry was confirmed later in the year when the Idaho Mining Association bragged in its annual report that "we enjoy quick and convenient access to the Governor on all matters of interest to the industry."

In early summer the Greater Sawtooth Preservation Council made public its findings on how best to protect the White Clouds. The plan called for the establishment of a 1.3 million acre Greater Sawtooth National Park and National Recreation Area complex modeled after the successful North Cascades plan. The lowland areas surrounding the Sawtooth, White Cloud, Boulder, Pioneer, and Smoky Ranges would be classified as National Recreation Area, while the upland reaches of these mountains would become national park units. All lands, both Park and NRA, would be withdrawn from mineral entry and the whole complex would be administered by the National Park Service, whose record for protection against mining encroachment has been excellent.

Legislative proposals to protect this region extend back more than half a century, focusing mainly on the spectacular Sawtooth Mountains and adjacent Stanley Basin. At various times National Park status was proposed, but vigorous opposition by powerful exploitative interests prevented passage of any such legislation. The rugged Sawtooth Range remained largely free of encroachment because some 200,000 acres there are classified as a Forest Service Primitive Area, but Stanley Basin is another matter. About 22,000 acres of this valley comprise privately owned ranchland which land speculators began

buying up in the early 1960's for summer home sub-
divisions. Spurred by the threat of such destructive developments, Senators Frank Church and Len Jordan spon-
sored legislation calling for a joint Forest Service-Na-
tional Park Service study of the area to determine the best
means of protection. Two separate plans were considered,
a National Park and a Forest Service administered National Recreation Area. Either would embrace the Sawtooth Range and Stanley Basin. Both would retain the
mountains as wilderness.

In June of 1966, a hearing was held in Sun Valley by
the Senate Interior and Insular Affairs Subcommittee, to
receive public opinion on both proposals. The majority of
testimony was anti-park. At that time, conservationists
were not well organized in the state. The Idaho Alpine
Club and the Idaho Wildlife Federation were active, but
there was no Greater Sawtooth Preservation Council, no
Idaho Environmental Council, or Hells Canyon Preservation Council. So-called multiple-use interests, on the other
hand, were well organized, apparently due to the efforts
of the U. S. Forest Service, which stood to lose lands
under its management if a park proposal should pass.
Field personnel of this agency were in a position to lobby
against the park because of their day-to-day contact with
local ranchers, loggers, community leaders, and businessmen. It did not take much to spur anti-park sentiment,
but the Forest Service appeared to work extra hard in
frightening local people with the spectre of "locking up"
the resources with a national park. One conservationist
in the Ketchum area told of a "Paul Revere" ride made by
the forest supervisor and his district rangers to get local
people to attend the hearing and fight the park. It paid
off, for most people at the hearing gave strong support to

the Forest Service multiple-use management under the National Recreation Area.

The Forest Service NRA proposal is a rather deceptive concept, perhaps best described as an empty caricature of a national park, designed to appease more than to preserve. Purporting to protect the area, in reality the NRA proposal would probably step up its destruction by developing its national prominence without the protective features and administration of a national park. Far worse, conservationists feel, the NRA would deceptively lull people into believing that the area is protected when, in reality, the Forest Service may carry on business as usual, with logging and road building, for example. And under this NRA designation, mining could continue unabated.

In addition, provisions in the Forest Service NRA bill were too weak to protect adequately Stanley Basin from proliferating summer home ghettos. The National Park Service, on the other hand, has had much experience administering private lands existing within park boundaries.

The GSPC proposal calls for administration of the entire Park and National Recreation Area complex by the National Park Service, and differs markedly from the Forest Service NRA in that logging and mining would be banned. Designating the lowland areas Park Service NRA rather than National Park units constituted a concession to sportsmen so they could continue to hunt there, since hunting is barred in National Parks. The National Park units embrace the vulnerable high country of not only the Sawtooth and White Cloud ranges, but the wild and spectacular Pioneer, Boulder, and Smoky Mountains as well. All of the National Park units would be earmarked for eventual inclusion in the Wilderness System, thus insuring the best possible protection for these areas not only from mining, but also from any future development. The 1.3 million acre complex is an exciting—and controversial—proposal. Perhaps its best endorsement has been the continual condemnation of the plan by the mining interests for they know that all mining would be banned. In a speech, the executive secretary of the Idaho Mining Association warned that the Forest Service NRA may make the miner "an endangered species," but asserted that if the park bill were to pass the miner would become "extinct."

With growing public concern over the threat to the White Clouds, Senators Church and Jordan and Congressman Orval Hansen amended the respective Senate and House NRA bills to include the White Clouds. But the gesture was weak, for the bill retained all its flaws. Management of the NRA was to remain in the hands of the Forest Service, for one thing. More importantly, however, Section 6 of that bill continued to read:

> Nothing in this Act shall effect the applicability *of the United States mining and mineral leasing laws on the federally owned lands within the recreation area,* except that all mining claims located or leases issued after the effective date of this Act shall be subject to regulation the Secretary [of Agriculture] *may* prescribe to effectuate the purposes of this Act. . . . (emphasis added)

Claim staking and the threat of more mines would thus continue in the area. The Senate subsequently passed the bill in the summer of 1969, but no action was taken in the House.

In a private meeting that summer with Greater Sawtooth Preservation Council directors, Senator Church indicated that the Forest Service National Recreation Area bill was the best that could be hoped for, given the state's current political climate. "A national park for the Sawtooth area is just not a political reality," he told the group, citing opposition to a park proposal at the 1966 hearings in Sun Valley. Conservationists argued that the whole environmental climate had changed radically since 1966 and there was now undoubtedly more support for a park. But to the surprise and disappointment of the assembled environmentalists, the once-crusading Senator remained unconvinced, reiterating his stance of pushing "realistic" legislation. Coming from such an experienced and respected statesman, the opinion could hardly be challenged. There was nothing to do but acquiesce. Within a single hour of one summer evening, the battle seemed over before it had hardly begun.

One man, however, was convinced that a park bill could and must be passed. Russell Brown, then vice president of the Council, later wrote, "Our Congressmen and newspaper editors all tell us that we aren't facing political realities, that we are politically naive. But the realities of yesterday are *dead* and of *no concern;* they are as empty as a miner's promise. What does concern us is the political reality of tomorrow, for therein lies the hope of relief from the Faustian bargain that man has been making with his environment. If a Sawtooth National Park requires a hard, uphill fight, so be it. *We must make it happen!"*

Exactly one year later, Senator Church and his colleagues would introduce a national park bill.

The events leading up to a major political upset are not easy to analyze, even in retrospect. If the U.S. voter seems capricious and difficult to predict, the Idaho voter

is impossible. Strongly conservative, Idahoans neverthe-
less frequently defy categorizing. In 1966 they turned
out a moderate three-term governor and elected a hard-
line Republican conservative, Don Samuelson. For the
U.S. Senate, a solid conservative Republican, Len Jordan, was elected. And yet, two years later, in his bid
for a third term, Frank Church, an anti-war conservationist and liberal Democrat, won an easy victory over
his conservative opponent.

In 1970, an election year involving the gubernatorial
seat, the incredible battle of words continued between
the governor on the one hand and the conservationists
and several major newspapers on the other. The allegedly
"hysterical preservationists" were, in fact, quite cool and
factual in their arguments. It was the governor who in-
dulged in hyperbole. "If we are going to allow the Sierra
Club and Alpine Club people to lock up our lands for
conservation purposes, then our trained college people
must be content with making beds at $1.25 per hour,"
Samuelson said. And his attorney general, Robert Rob-
son, made light of preserving the beauty of the state:
"An underground miner bringing home $47 a day is
beauty." (He neglected to mention, however, just where
miners were making $12,000 per year. The average an-
nual wage for miners in Idaho is less than $5,000, and
even a casual observer can see that towns in the mining
districts of Idaho are hardly the picture of affluence.)

During 1970, support continued to grow for the National Park-National Recreation Area complex. The
Greater Sawtooth Preservation Council, the Idaho Environmental Council, and other citizen groups worked
hard to gain public support for it through press releases,
public appearances, and slide shows, pointing out on

every occasion that this proposal would afford the best
long-term protection for the White Clouds and adjacent
areas. Publicly there seemed to be a growing suspicion
that the Forest Service NRA bill would not properly
preserve the region. Such suspicion was fed by the continual, active endorsement of the bill by logging and
mining interests.

In early August the break came. The House Interior
and Insular Affairs Committee announced that a public
hearing would be held by the Subcommittee on Parks
and Recreation later that month in Sun Valley. Following swiftly on the heels of that announcement came
word that in Washington the Idaho Congressional delegation had introduced respective House and Senate bills
calling for the establishment of a 750,000-acre national
park for the Sawtooth, White Cloud, and Boulder Mountains. It wasn't all that conservationists had hoped for
(the bills omitted the Pioneer Mountains), but it was a
starting point for public discussion. The hearing thus as-
sumed tremendous importance. It was now or never for
the White Clouds and environs.

The exploitative interests and the Forest Service also
realized the importance of this hearing. In a frenzy of
activity, conservationists and exploiters alike rallied
their respective forces to attend and testify. Like an
army readying for an encounter, each group prepared its
troops and planned strategies. The exploiters clearly
held the edge, with corporate funds and full-time em-
ployees disposed to muster their allies, whereas conservationists had to rely on contributions and volunteer
workers.

The subcommittee, not anticipating great public interest, scheduled but a single day for the hearing. Three

days would have been a more realistic minimum, for 367 people formally applied in writing to present testimony, a number surpassed in the history of that full House Committee on only two other occasions, the hearings on the North Cascades and Redwood National Park proposals.

The hearing bordered on chaos as the Opera House in Sun Valley filled to overflowing. Even running witnesses through at the rate of one every sixty seconds in two separate and simultaneous sessions did not afford opportunity for all to be heard. Nonetheless, by the time the hearing closed, those who favored the GSPC Park-NRA complex were clearly in the majority. It was a definite mandate for stronger action to save the region, a dramatic reversal of the attitudes expressed at the 1966 hearing.

Much of the testimony was predictable. The mining and timber industry confirmed their support for "multiple-use management" under the Forest Service NRA proposal. "We are convinced that our industry would not be permitted any type of entry or operation in a national park," testified A. J. Teske of the Idaho Mining Association. Another industry spokesman, from a California mining corporation, said, "A mine cannot be economically operated within a park under park regulations even if existing valid mineral rights or land ownerships are recognized." Right on, responded conservationists.

Governor Samuelson did not make an appearance but sent, instead, six representatives on behalf of the state, in an apparent attempt to monopolize the hearing. Subcommittee Chairman Roy Taylor finally had to gavel out of order the executive director of the Idaho Department of Commerce and Development when he persisted in trying to read a 30-minute statement while other citizens were being strictly limited to one minute.

It also seemed clear that the Forest Service had once again expended great lobbying effort to retain its domain. Many local residents, apparently so informed by the Forest Service, expressed fear that a national park and NRA complex would mean an end to private ownership within its boundaries, with the result that church camps would be condemned and destroyed, and grazing would be halted. Conservationists pointed out that such contentions were absurd.

The hearing also became the focal point for the real beginning of the Idaho gubernatorial race. Governor Samuelson reiterated his strong pro-mining and development stance. So strong, in fact, was his support of the mining proposal that he would not even back the weak Forest Service NRA, calling instead for a "study" of the situation.

The newly selected Democratic candidate for governor, State Senator Cecil Andrus, appeared personally at the hearing and strongly supported the GSPC Park-NRA plan. Andrus had emerged the victor from a three-way Democratic primary after receiving endorsement from the Idaho Environmental Council and other conservationists. The battle lines were thus sharply drawn; perhaps no other political race in the nation was so clearly defined along environmental lines. As important as this hearing was for the public to express its approval of the Park-NRA proposal, the real consensus would emerge at the ballot box in November.

Between the August hearing and election day, conservationists threw themselves into the campaign for

Andrus. Even staunch Republicans who were conservationists worked hard for the Democrat, and it became an
all-or-nothing effort, because not only did the fate of the
White Clouds hang on the election, but other important
areas would be affected as well. Governor Samuelson
supported the damming of Hells Canyon, and his anti-
wilderness attitude would undoubtedly put development
pressures on such places as the Idaho Primitive Area
scheduled for reclassification, possibly as an addition to
the Wilderness System. His attorney general had already
challenged the Wild River status of the Middle Fork of
the Salmon River, contending that the river belonged to
the state for "development" purposes.

For most of the conservationists this was their first real
involvement in politics. Many of them became accomplished campaigners in a wide range of activities, from
public rallies to door-to-door stumping. It was an incredible effort on the part of a rag-tag bunch of inexperi-
enced idealists who were crazy enough to think they
could win.

In the closing days of the campaign, Governor Samuelson continued to insist that the proposed mine was not in
the White Clouds at all. The *Idaho Daily Statesman,*
largest and most influential newspaper in the state, neatly
put to rest that absurdity once and for all: "The governor
has the mine in the White Clouds when he's talking about
'lock ups'. He moves it outside the White Clouds when
he talks about the impact of mining in the area.

"So far most of the controversy about the mine has
been based on the assumption that it was stationary. Few
realized that it was a portable mine.

"A lot of people have the impression that the mine is

located in a picturesque valley just below Castle Peak, which is the biggest and most beautiful mountain in the White Clouds. They are also laboring under the illusion that the mine is stationary, would involve a huge open pit, millions of tons of tailings and might pollute the East Fork of the Salmon River.

"There are thousands of acres of Idaho landscape of far less quality than the area near Castle Peak, with much less potential for polluting salmon streams.

"If the mine is really portable, all the governor has to do is move it to another location."

In an overt attempt to intimidate the Idaho Environmental Council, the governor asked the attorney general to determine whether a non-profit organization could legally endorse a political candidate. The attorney general had to report, in embarrassment and in public, that it was, indeed, legal.

Day after day Idaho newspapers carried front page releases and statements from the governor. And day after day came refutations of Samuelson's allegations by the Greater Sawtooth Preservation Council, the Idaho Environmental Council, and other citizen groups.

All in all it was an incredible campaign, and as election day drew near even the governor's backers from the mining industry apparently grew uncomfortable over the intemperance and absurdity of his public statements. That, at least, would explain the uncharacteristic silence which suddenly fell upon the governor's office. It was too late, however.

On November 5, Cecil Andrus was elected Governor of Idaho, the first Democrat to be elected to that office in 25 years. The Andrus victory was the second mandate,

stronger yet than the first, for the full protection of the
White Cloud-Sawtooth country by means of the National
Park-National Recreation Area complex.

In 1971 conservationists expected Idaho's Congressional delegation, armed now with two strong mandates,
to act quickly on the Park-NRA proposal. Not only was
action slow in coming; one of the worst turnarounds in
Idaho politics and national conservation annals was in
the offing. After long silence, Senators Church and Jordan
and Congressmen McClure and Hansen announced in
March the introduction of a *Sawtooth National Recreation Area bill*. No park. No protection.

Conservationists were shocked. "Bad news in a new
wrapping," said the Greater Sawtooth Preservation Council. Russ Brown, now the President of GSPC, sum-
marized the conservationists' reaction by stating, "The
Sawtooth NRA bill offers but a hint of a whisper of a
promise of protection. The miners are happy again and
looking forward, after a discreet delay of a few years, to
a few decades of fun and profit while practicing their own
unique style of landscape architecture. The Forest Service
feels secure in the knowledge that it has once more used
public finds to defy the public will, thus retaining management control of the empire. The destruction of the
White Clouds will be the price we all will pay for Forest
Service dominion.

*"If the purpose of the NRA bill is the protection of
the Greater Sawtooth area, it is a failure; if the purpose
is to make people believe it is protected, it is a fraud.*

"The best that the NRA bill offers the White Clouds
is an indecent burial."

Conservationists demanded an explanation of the turnabout. In private, Senator Church admitted that he was in favor of "stronger legislation," but said that Congressman McClure was opposed to a park plan which would preclude mining. McClure, whose district includes most of the mining areas of Idaho, has long been a supporter of mining and logging and a foe to conservation. And with McClure on the House Interior Committee, through which the legislation must pass, the NRA bill was the best that could be hoped for under the circumstances, according to Church. Conservationists were bitterly disappointed that the senator would give in on this issue without a fight.

As if to underscore the Forest Service's lobbying role, shortly after the introduction of the NRA bill that agency began a series of spot radio commercials in the Idaho Falls area. These commercials stated that "a National Recreation Area is favored for the Sawtooths" (by whom, they didn't say). The ads also contained subtle anti-park propaganda. It was thus becoming apparent that a strong coalition was being formed between industry and the federal agency.

In early June the House Subcommittee on Parks and Recreation scheduled another hearing, this one in Washington, D.C. An interesting bit of behind-the-scenes maneuvering shortly before the hearing emphasized the efforts of exploitative forces to circumvent the two mandates from Idaho citizens. The Department of Interior had prepared testimony which recommended a Park-NRA plan. Within two days, however, Interior's statement was suddenly changed so that it now supported the weak Forest Service NRA bill under consideration. Subsequent inquiries revealed that Congressman Hansen had apparently exerted pressure through the White House to force the department to change its stance. Hansen's collaborator, it seems, was Mary Brooks, director of the U.S. Mint. Mrs. Brooks, a native Idahoan with family grazing interests in the Sawtooth region, would seem only too happy to help kill park support. *She had, in fact, testified personally at the 1966 Senate hearing against the national park proposal, supporting "multiple use in mining and lumbering and livestock."* In this way the Nixon administration came to take a stand counter to the wishes of a majority of Idahoans.

With the Department of Interior thus disciplined, the hearing went as expected. Only three conservationists from Idaho could afford the trip to Washington, while numerous people representing mining, logging, and grazing interests attended.

Congressman McClure, out of direct sight of his constituents, was hostile to the conservationists during the hearing, arguing with them over points of philosophy for protection and defending the mining interests. The hearing was a clear victory for the multiple-use interests. "If you listen carefully, you can hear the sound of bulldozers starting up," said one angry conservationist afterward.

A few months after the hearing, Congressman Hansen sent a questionnaire to his constituents asking their opinion on the proposal for the Sawtooth-White Cloud region. It should have made him reflect a moment on his political future when he discovered that, of the thousands who responded, support for the GSPC Park-NRA complex led by a two-to-one margin.

About four miles from the base of Castle Peak, Little Boulder Creek breaks out of a steep, wooded valley into a large grassy meadow. The icy stream meanders here, its sparkling clear water split into several ribbons that wind through willows and marshes in a silvery lacework. The meadow, green and lush in August, is splashed with color by asters and arnica and Indian paintbrush. Directly south and west, the craggy, snow-covered spire of Castle Peak rises sharply within the framework of two sloping hillsides. The Tetons, Wind Rivers, Sawtooths, and Cascades notwithstanding, this scene of meadow and stream and mountain is one of the most beautiful in the nation.

The meadow lies approximately in the center of the proposed mine tailings pond. The broad catenary formed by the sloping, wooded hillsides to the south marks the edge of the open pit. Standing in the middle of this alpine meadow, one cannot easily visualize dirty gray slurry covering the grass and flowers and stream to a depth of several hundred feet; nor is it easy to picture the white open wound of rock freshly exposed by an open pit or the slash of a road through forest, or the pall of smoke from a mill.

Standing here, one senses the enchantment gradually drain away, replaced by a knot tightening deep in the pit of the stomach, a knot of fear and rage and panic and despair. For it is clear that the destruction of the White Clouds will ultimately be caused not merely by bulldozers and dynamite, but by something more basic and dangerous: legislative irresponsibility. Four men have it within their power to save this place once and for all, but they have chosen not to do so. The mandates have been clear. For the most part, Idaho's congressmen and senators have chosen to ignore them. To his credit, Senator Church has recently worked hard to strengthen the weaknesses of the NRA bill. Whether this is enough, only time will tell. Senator Jordan seemed simply not to care since he was to retire in '72. Congressmen McClure and Hansen argue, socratically, that they cannot push for a park because it is difficult to obtain. In reality, the difficulty of attainment arises because they do not want a park.

The Forest Service NRA bill was passed by the House of Representatives. The Senate version, strengthened by Senator Church's amendments, has also passed. But these amendments may very likely be watered down or killed in conference committee by Representative McClure and Congressman Wayne Aspinall, both allies of the mining industry.

ASARCO's claims have been neither validated nor patented—yet. Since these lands are still in federal ownership, a park bill could withdraw them from mineral entry and, even though the miners lay claim to them, the claim could probably never be patented because a "prudent man" would be deemed unlikely to mine them in a national park. This way, these lands could become part of a park without great expenditure of funds to buy patents from the mining companies.

At this writing there is a temporary standoff. There is no mine, but neither is there a park. Still, as in the Hells Canyon standoff, other destructive activities continue to erode the region. The Forest Service has continued to encourage motorized intrusion of the White Cloud wilderness by trailbikes, apparently in the hope of building a larger anti-park and anti-wilderness following. Trailbikes are tearing up meadows and trails, shattering peace and tranquillity with the roar of their strident engines. Moreover, the latest inventory shows forty-six separate mining and prospecting activities in the White Cloud-Boulder-Pioneer Mountain region. Claims are even being staked in the Sawtooth Primitive Area now. And the sale of subdivided land continues in Stanley Basin.

Along the east edge of that alpine meadow runs a trail next to which someone has driven a tall wooden stake with a fluttering, fluorescent red streamer. The stake, as stakes go, seems very ordinary. In reality it is quite eloquent, for it tells the passerby, *what is yours will soon be ours. By means of an antiquated law and with help from your elected representatives in Congress, we shall soon appropriate and desecrate. And when we are through, we will move on, looking for more such wilderness.*

Or, as American Smelting and Refining Company says: "Certainly we're going to make a big hole."

*The Snake River*

*Castle Peak, White Cloud
Mountains*

*Lodgepole pine forest,*
*Yellowstone National Park*

*Alpine Lake, Sawtooth*
*Primitive Area*

*Ground detail, cedar forest
along the Lochsa River*

*High in the Tetons*

*Lichens on lava, Craters of the
Moon National Monument*

*Aspen in autumn, Teton
National Park*

# 5. The Magruder Corridor

In the beginning wilderness surrounded man, engulfing him with immensity. Today the inverse is true. We surround and dominate the few remaining pockets of wilderness, held at bay by tenuous laws, arbitrary boundaries, and, occasionally, conscience.

Even the growing number of Americans who have tasted the challenge of wilderness and sampled its values may find it difficult to comprehend a land so wild that it still surrounds and sometimes engulfs. Too many of those protected pockets are pitifully small. Of the 88 areas in the National Wilderness Preservation System, perhaps one-third can be traversed in a single day's hike. Climb to the top of rugged peaks and you may observe, rather than an ocean of wilderness, a sea of smog. Much of our wilderness is more vertical than horizontal, often the bare leftovers of snow and rock for which exploiters had no immediate use. Beautiful and rugged though they may be, these places are hardly representative of the great expanse and great ecological diversities of unspoiled lands that once were.

If one were to devise a test for wilderness, perhaps the simplest and most revealing would be darkness. There are not many places left in the country where one can command a nighttime view of a sweeping landscape and fail to see the glimmer—sometimes the glare—of electric lights. And where there is light there is man. And wires and roads and towns.

But from a ridge separating the Salmon and Selway rivers in central Idaho, such a view is possible.

On a star-filled night with but a sliver of a moon, there is more than ample light to discern the shape and features of the land. To the south it slides away in a smooth plunge to meet the Salmon River 5,000 feet below. The big river is not visible from here, but its presence is etched deeply into the grain of the country. Shadowy and silvery mountain forms recede far to the south and west and east and both the dim light and the forest give them a velvet-like texture.

Turn 180 degrees and the land rolls away in still more sweeping forms. The great gulf carved by the Selway, while not as deep as the gorge of the Salmon, is equally apparent. Ridge after ridge recedes into the pale distance. From the Salmon River Mountains to the Bitterroots, from the Bighorn Crags to unnamed peaks, from rounded hills to yawning valleys and gorges, in almost 2,000 square miles of land to be seen in a 360-degree panorama, there is not a single light to indicate the presence of man.

Wilderness.

In most ways it is a soft land, more reminiscent of the forest-cloaked hills and mountains of the Appalachians than of the Rocky Mountains. A sea of green pitches and tosses, and only to the northeast in the Bitterroots are whitecaps of bare rock and snow common. From valley to mountain top it is an almost unbroken expanse of lush verdure, perhaps the largest remaining expanse of wilderness forest left in these lower 48 states.

On the divide separating it from the Salmon drainage, the Selway River begins amid alpine fir, gathers waters from hillsides of lodgepole pine, tumbles into valleys lined with monarchs of ponderosa pine and Douglas fir; farther on, cedars shade the crystalline waters. Though not a big river, the Selway is substantial enough, rushing more than 100 miles before it joins the Lochsa and the two become the Clearwater. It is probably the only sizable river system in the lower 48 still largely intact from headwaters to mouth. Virtually the entire watershed is wilderness, with little in the way of man's intrusions. During peak runoff of winter's snow, a time when most rivers and streams are choked with silt and mud washed from roaded and logged watersheds, the Selway runs clear. The way a river should.

Of interest to naturalists is the fact that the region apparently escaped general glaciation during the Ice Age, and thus certain plants and animals found here may have survived the Pleistocene with little or no disturbance.

For centuries—in fact, for perhaps several thousand years—there was a clearly defined route from the Bitterroot Valley of Montana to western Idaho, traversing the upper reaches of the Selway River. Lewis and Clark heard of this Nez Perce trail from their Indian guides, but chose another Indian route crossing the Idaho panhandle farther north, following the Lochsa River. Mountain men explored the region later, but apparently it held no riches for them in beaver furs. When prospectors and miners arrived, following gold strikes in the Salmon River country, the upper Selway was combed for minerals, but again it held disappointment for fortune-seekers. A spur trail developed off the old Nez Percé track and led to the mines along the Salmon; it was used frequently by packers and merchants traveling between the mines and such towns as Elk City in north-central Idaho. And it was on this trail, not far from where it crosses the Selway, that a packer from Lewiston, Lloyd Magruder, was robbed and murdered by a gang of bandits in 1863, the year Idaho became a territory.

Prospectors and miners came and went, but the wilderness changed little. In time the region was included among the thirteen forest reserves established by Presidential proclamation in 1897. Acting under the Forest Reserve Act of 1891, President Grover Cleveland set aside more than 21 million acres of forests for conservation purposes. Eight years later, with the creation of the U.S. Forest Service, this area was divided between the Nez Perce and Bitterroot national forests.

For the first twenty or so years the upper Selway country remained little affected by the management policies of the U.S. Forest Service. But growing within the agency was the philosophy that certain lands should be preserved untouched for the sake of wildlife and other values. Leader of this school was Aldo Leopold, and as a result of his influence an area in the Gila National Forest of New Mexico, comprising more than a half million acres, was set aside in 1924 as the first land in the nation to be preserved purely as wilderness.

But interest in wilderness preservation was not confined solely to federal agencies. In 1930 a group of farsighted Idaho citizens, led by Governor H. C. Baldridge, recom-

mended to the Forest Service that a vast area south of
the Salmon River be protected against road-building, logging, and other encroachments. The next year the agency
established the 1.2-million-acre Idaho Primitive Area, a
land of untracked mountains, pure streams, and wild
rivers. Contained within it are the Middle Fork of the
Salmon River, the Bighorn Crags, and a multitude of
mountains and lakes where, even today, only a few men
have ever set foot.

In 1936 the Forest Service established a 1.8-million-
acre Selway-Bitterroot Primitive Area, another expanse of
wild and beautiful country that included virtually the
entire watershed of the Selway River plus the Bitterroot
Range. The Selway-Bitterroot extended north from the
Salmon River all the way to the Lochsa River and east to
the Bitterroot Valley of Montana. With a topography
ranging from 1,600 feet along the lower Selway to more
than 10,000 feet in the Bitterroots, it contained an incredible diversity of plants and animals. Together with the
Idaho Primitive Area to the south, it formed (and still
does) the largest contiguous wilderness in the then 48
states—3 million acres in size, more than 150 miles long,
with hundreds of miles of wild streams and rivers. A region roughly the size of the state of Connecticut, it was
(and is) as wild and unspoiled as when Lewis and Clark
first passed nearby.

It did not seem destined to remain so for long.

In 1939 an effort was made by the Forest Service to
strengthen the vague regulations under which primitive
areas were administered. Largely through the efforts of
Robert Marshall, chief of the Division of Recreation and
Lands and the agency's leading crusader for wilderness,
new provisions were adopted for the establishment of

wilderness areas. Under the new classification, rules were more specific in such matters as road-building and logging, both of which were prohibited. The Forest Service also called for a review of all established primitive areas for possible inclusion in the more protective classification. But because of World War II, these reviews and reclassifications were postponed for several years.

When the agency resumed these studies after the war, conservationists became increasingly concerned over the fate of the Selway-Bitterroot Primitive Area. Particularly disturbing was the gathering evidence that the Forest Service planned to exclude a large area in the reclassification from primitive to wilderness area. The new regulations governing the establishment of wilderness areas expressly prohibited roads. Unfortunately, a primitive road had been built in 1934 for fire-fighting purposes. Crossing the upper Selway drainage, from Hamilton, Montana, to Elk City, Idaho, the road traversed the management unit known as the Magruder Ranger District.

Conservationists feared the road would provide the rationale for excluding unnecessarily large areas from wilderness designation. To close the road was obviously difficult since use had increased over the years and improvements had been made. In consultation with the Forest Service, conservationists recommended in 1956 that the area north of the road be added to the soon-to-be-established Selway-Bitterroot Wilderness Area, and that the region to the south, all the way to the Salmon River, be added to the Idaho Primitive Area, the whole to become the River of No Return Wilderness Area. The road, then, would be a narrow strip separating these two great wilderness domains. And, except for this ribbon, the area would remain largely protected.

The Forest Service, however, had some different ideas. In 1960 the agency announced its proposal. Recommended was a 1,164,000-acre Selway–Bitterroot Wilderness Area, a cut of half a million acres in size from the original primitive area. The largest single deletion was some 292,000 acres that included the upper Selway drainage. Most of this area was known as the Magruder Corridor and contained the road in question and much of the surrounding upper Selway country. All of these deletions were to be placed in regular multiple-use category, meaning they would be open to logging, road-building, or other developments.

In early 1961 the Forest Service held hearings on this reclassification proposal. Conservationists sharply criticized the plan, pointing out that such a large deletion was not warranted merely on the existence of the Magruder road. A plea was once more made to limit this deletion to a narrow corridor paralleling the road and putting the rest, north and south of it, into wilderness designation. George Marshall, brother of the late Robert Marshall, representing the Sierra Club at the hearings, zeroed in on the absurdity of the Forest Service proposal: "There is a great difference between an existing simple and informal road winding through the mountains with natural conditions extending out from the road, and the creation of a 20-mile multiple-use gap between the two great areas of wilderness."

The Forest Service proposal created much controversy, both for and against. Before the records were closed the views of some 4,000 individuals and organizations were recorded either by letter or petition. The opinions they expressed were roughly split, with those opposed to the large deletions having somewhat of an edge.

As a result of the tremendous interest, the Forest Service began to review its own decision and consider the recommendations offered at the hearings. In early 1963 Secretary of Agriculture Orville L. Freeman announced the results: the establishment of a 1,240,000-acre Selway–Bitterroot Wilderness Area—an increase over the 1960 proposal of less than seven percent. In addition, a 217,-000-acre Salmon River Breaks Primitive Area was established. Originally a part of the old Selway–Bitterroot Primitive Area, this new unit lay north of and immediately adjacent to the Salmon River. However, the large area including the Magruder Corridor that lay between the two was declassified from wilderness to multiple-use management. It was a defeat for conservation forces. Nearly half a million acres of wilderness had been lost.

In historical perspective, one can trace recent national controversy over Forest Service management practices back to the beginning of the Magruder Corridor controversy. It was probably this one issue that triggered the polarization and mistrust that conservationists developed over Forest Service management motives. For once the decision was reached, the agency turned a deaf ear on citizen appeals, and the arrogance displayed by Forest Service officials provoked anger among conservationists.

It almost seems a corollary to Parkinson's Law that federal land management agencies expand their activities ultimately to destroy all remaining wilderness. By dictum and by bureaucratic inertia it appears inevitable that, left to their own devices, agencies such as the National Park Service and the U.S. Forest Service would eventually tame and develop every square foot of their respective domains. To manage is to manipulate. The more managers the more manipulation. Increasingly, the Forest Service has come to be viewed by many as a massive welfare program for forestry school graduates, a place where foresters may practice their newly acquired knowledge of manipulative techniques.

As an arm of the Department of Agriculture, the Forest Service is administrator of some 187 million acres of public lands, a trusteeship embracing a large proportion of what remains of America's unspoiled lands. The man primarily responsible for the establishment of the national forests, Gifford Pinchot, did not expressly wish to preserve them, but rather wanted to save these forests from the reckless saws of monopolistic timber barons. Pinchot was a forester and a social reformer. But he was not a conservationist of the Thoreau and Muir philosophy. He felt these forests reserves should be utilized for the benefit of man and that strict preservation without utilization was wasteful. His rationale lay in the basic and traditional tenets of forestry: trees are a renewable resource, and with proper management, forests can be made to yield a perpetual crop.

The protection or preservation philosophy emerged slowly, in the early days of the Forest Service, but through the efforts of such men as Aldo Leopold and Robert Marshall the agency began to establish a system of wilderness preserves where land and life cycles were left unimpaired. Critics from both within and without argued in the utilitarian vein that these preserves were far larger and far more numerous than they needed to be. The utilitarians ultimately won out. With time the agency began gradually to whittle away the size of these preserves. This erosion of protected wilderness was spurred by a subtle transition in the philosophy of the nation's forestry

schools. Michael Frome, perhaps the most apt student of
the Forest Service, sums it up best:

"In direct reflection of the Theodore Roosevelt policies,
Pinchot had spoken of the evils of monopoly and special
privilege, the needs of equal opportunity, the values of
setting the common good of all above the private gain
of a few. Forestry schools turned out a breed of idealists
determined to halt the anarchic, free-wheeling destruction
of the forests by the timber barons and to rescue the
overexploited range from the cattlemen.

"Those were other days. A review of history shows that
following World War II a new breed emerged. Foresters
generally no longer reflected the social crusade, but the
industrial demand for production of wood fiber and cellu-
lose. Practicality in due course replaced idealism. The
forestry schools responded with emphasis on cost-con-
sciousness, on getting every forest acre working to its full
capacity, training a corps of professionals tuned to economics rather than to environmental protection for the
benefit of future generations."

Frome's analysis is reinforced by an examination of
contemporary forestry schools where curricula are frequently studded with course titles containing such words
as "utilization," "economics," "valuation," and "management." These "hard" or practical courses make up the major portion of those required; environmental, ecological,
or recreation courses are often relegated to elective status.

As land managers, foresters often display both contempt for beauty and ignorance of the functional relation-
ships in untouched biological communities. Thus, a grace-
ful old tree becomes "overmature," and a virgin wilderness
forest containing all natural stages of life, death, decay

and renewal is referred to as a "decadent" stand of timber. From an ecological standpoint such terms are absurd. But in an economic framework they provide the rationale for manipulating forest lands for maximum timber yield.

The forestry schools produced foresters for not only the Forest Service but for industry as well, and all were steeped in the same general philosophy. It thus seemed inevitable that an incestuous relationship would develop between the wood products industry and the land managers. With support of the agency, industry argues that *not* cutting trees is wasteful practice and such wood is needed by the nation. As in so many resource areas, however, these "needs" are largely created by the advertising resources of the industry, and over the years the national forests have come to be considered by industry as a cheap and easy source of raw materials. Environmental and social costs were (and are) largely ignored. As long as the Forest Service is willing to sell off the national forests cheaply, there will be no impetus to develop efficient waste recycling of wood and paper products or to develop and advertise alternatives to the use of wood in construction.

Faced with an agency increasingly hostile to wilderness preservation, conservationists began to press for legislation to establish a National Wilderness Preservation System, one that would be free of the vagaries of bureaucracies. The first Wilderness Bill was introduced in Congress in 1956, but there were many years of hard battle before it became a reality. Finally, in 1964, President Lyndon Johnson signed into law the Wilderness Act, designating 54 areas to receive immediate protection and calling for a ten-year review of 34 Forest Service primitive areas as possible additions to the National Wilderness Preservation

System. The Selway–Bitterroot was one of those units granted immediate protection. But the fate of the Magruder Corridor had, if anything, become more complicated by the passage of the Wilderness Act, for in order to protect it, conservationists would now have to seek Congressional action.

In the fall of 1964 the Forest Service seemed bent on the full development of the Magruder Corridor. Some observers thought the agency was acting with deliberate haste in order to prevent any reconsideration of wilderness status. Road construction and reconstruction plans were moving ahead, and timber sales were in the offing. Spurred by these threats, conservationists began to organize and coordinate efforts. In the Bitterroot Valley a group of citizens formed the Save the Upper Selway Committee, spearheaded by Mrs. Doris Milner and aided by G. M. Brandborg, retired former supervisor of the Bitterroot National Forest. Mrs. Milner and her family had for many years enjoyed the wilderness recreation offered by the upper Selway country. Brandborg had fought hard for the protection of the area during his years with the Forest Service. In Idaho the North Idaho Wilderness Committee, led by Morton Brigham of Lewiston, was already a functioning organization. The two groups began to formulate plans for protecting the corridor from the imminent threat of chain saws and bulldozers.

Backing the conservationists were a growing number of fish and game experts who feared for the purity of the Selway if logging was allowed in the drainage, where steep hillsides and fragile granitic soils would produce disastrous erosion and silting in what is one of the nation's last unspoiled rivers.

The determined efforts of the local groups brought the

controversy to the attention of conservationists on a regional and national scale. The result was an increasing volume of mail protesting the Forest Service plans to the Secretary of Agriculture and to the congressmen and senators of both Idaho and Montana. The Forest Service response was a campaign to enlist the support of exploitative interests. The Bitterroot National Forest supervisor recommended to his staff that they contact such groups as the Northwest Mining Association, Western Wood Products Industries, the Inland Empire Multiple Use Committee (a front group for several timber companies), and power companies and grazing interests in an effort to counteract the growing citizen concern.

In addition to these lobbying efforts, the Forest Service also published a brochure describing the multiple-use plans for the Magruder Corridor, touting the improved recreation and transportation, with major emphasis on the economic benefits from timber harvest. The brochure committed the Forest Service totally to development of the Magruder Corridor. There were no indications that any other options were possible. Morton Brigham angrily charged that the Forest Service "proposes to tear up one-quarter million acres of wilderness at a cost nobody knows to get less timber than it takes to operate one small sawmill." Bruce Bowler, a Boise attorney active in the Save the Upper Selway fight, said, "Never in my experience have I seen such persistence to perpetuate such a mistake notwithstanding all of the competent evidence against it."

Throughout 1964 and 1965, concern continued to mount over the calculated effort of the Forest Service to carry out its logging plans in the area. Hence Senators Lee Metcalf of Montana and Frank Church of Idaho secured from Secretary of Agriculture Freeman a precedent-setting appointment of a special, nongovernment study committee in August 1966. Headed by Dr. George Selke, a Montana educator and special consultant to the secretary, the committee included Dr. James Meiman, professor of watershed management at Colorado State University; Dr. Kenneth Davis, professor of forestry management at the University of Michigan; and William Reavley, western field representative for the National Wildlife Federation. After conservationists voiced fears over the makeup of the committee (Reavley had already publicly endorsed the Forest Service plans), two more appointments were made: Dr. Donald Obee, chairman of the Division of Life Sciences at Boise College, and Daniel Poole, secretary of the Wildlife Management Institute.

The appointment of the Selke Committee was only a partial and temporary victory for the conservation forces, for in addition to the doubt concerning the impartiality of it, the Secretary of Agriculture had charged the committee *only* with reviewing current Forest Service plans. It was specifically instructed *not* to reopen the original wilderness declassification decision. Despite these handicaps, conservationists were able to make a strong impression on the group.

After touring the area in question, the Selke Committee scheduled three public hearings—"meetings" they were called—in December 1966 to receive both citizen comment and opinions of experts. As a result of these meetings in Grangeville and Boise, Idaho, and Missoula, Montana, the committee compiled a total of more than 1,000 letters and statements; roughly two-thirds were opposed to the Forest Service plans. In personal statements before the group, numerous wildlife experts opposed the plans on the grounds of probable damage to both aquatic and terrestrial habitat.

The meetings once more brought together representatives of conflicting land-use views, and the public debate centered largely on economic value versus preservation. As in past and future confrontations, opponents of wilderness labeled these areas as "lockups," arguing that such preserves are inaccessible to large numbers, while development of the Magruder Corridor would "open up" the area to both recreation and economic uses. The mining industry claimed that national security was dependent on an expanded mineral supply and on these grounds opposed wilderness "lockups." The timber industry and Forest Service had waged a scare campaign in the Bitterroot Valley, warning of job losses and declining business if the corridor was not logged. Thus, local chambers of commerce and county commissioners supported the development plans.

Conservationists cited the relative scarcity of wilderness in the nation, while biologists and ecologists pointed to the scientific value of untouched areas. Subliminal to all these arguments, however, was the growing evidence that a land-managing bureaucracy—insensitive to public concern—had become increasingly dominated by an exploitative philosophy. The arrogant "trust-us-for-we-are-the-experts" attitude displayed by the Forest Service, and liberally reinforced by industry foresters, had alienated a growing number of people. As one observer pointed out, all land and resource experts are not in the employ of the Forest Service, and in recent years many such people have challenged judgment in the management decisions made by the agency.

In June 1967 the findings of the Selke Committee were
made public. Even in its mildest interpretation, the report
was a severe rebuke of the studies and decisions made by
the Forest Service. Lack of sufficient planning detail and
the absence of meaningful studies on the impact of development were two major criticisms. "Multiple use," the
report said, "as applied by the Forest Service, is a con-
structive concept, and a necessary statement of policy and
principles. But, at best, it should be regarded as only a
framework for approaching the complex problems of forest land management. It is not a formula for specific land-
use allocation in a particular area . . . Considerable
reliance is placed on rather arbitrary zoning that can par-
tition without integrative consideration of the area as a
whole. Resultant management decisions tend to follow the
same pattern as there is a strong tendency for each land
use to be applied following handbooks and manuals prepared for each use."

"Single use," the report added, "is also consistent with
the [Multiple Use] Act."

The committee concluded that there are three primary
values in the area:

• A strategic watershed as regards both water supply
and fish, constituting a major portion of the upper Selway
River.

• An historic and important natural connection between Idaho and Montana.

• A recreational area important particularly as pro-
viding an avenue of access to two great wilderness and
primitive areas of national significance.

Noting that "road-building constitutes the single greatest potential hazard to water values on the Magruder Corridor," the committee recommended deferment of timber

cutting and road construction until more specific and comprehensive evaluation is made on all the impacts and values of the area.

Despite the fact it was not to review the wilderness classification decision, the Selke Committee gave implicit endorsement to *de facto* wilderness management of the area: "The committee believes the Forest Service has in the Magruder Corridor, as elsewhere, an opportunity to demonstrate that, under unrestricted national forest classification, it can manage the land so that primary values can be balanced with several uses over an area as a whole. The Forest Service needs to strengthen public confidence that wildland areas can be managed for a primary use or uses without being specifically designated."

The report of the Selke Committee was far more favorable than conservationists had originally hoped for. "It is not often that an entrenched bureaucracy like the Forest Service is overruled in its own domain," said *The New York Times*. Most significant was that it brought about a temporary stay of execution for the Magruder Corridor. Conservationists were hopeful the Forest Service would use this opportunity to reconsider seriously their original declassification decision. And since the Selke Committee had found timber growing to be "marginal in financial terms," the agency would most logically agree to wilderness classification for the area.

Directed by the Secretary of Agriculture to carry out the recommendations of the Selke Report, the Forest Service began studies of the resources of the corridor. It soon became apparent, however, that the Service did not take the committee report seriously. The regional forester confided to one observer that he considered the study committee to be a delaying tactic perpetrated by preservation-

ists. Implicit in his attitude was the fact the Forest Service
did not intend to let the Selke Report interfere with its
plans. And as confirmation of that, Morton Brigham discovered in late 1967 that the Forest Service was planning
a 30-foot-wide "trail" between the corridor and the
Salmon River Breaks Primitive Area.

Conservationists renewed their appeal to Senators
Church and Metcalf to introduce legislation adding the
land north of the Magruder road to the Selway-Bitterroot
Wilderness Area, and the land south of the road to the
Salmon River Breaks Primitive Area. But the senators argued that the Forest Service studies should be completed
first to determine whether the agency planned to protect
the area itself.

In early 1970 the Forest Service published the results
of its studies as the Magruder Corridor Resource Inventory. The report contained no management recommendations. However, numerous recreation sites were identified
that would require extensive road construction throughout parts of the corridor, in some cases close to existing
wilderness or primitive area boundaries. Timber resources
were carefully documented and soils were identified as to
their stability. Almost half the area was classified as low
or moderate erosion hazard.

In late 1970 the bombshell was dropped. In a prelimi-
nary report entitled "Magruder Corridor General Management Direction," the Bitterroot National Forest supervisor recommended extensive logging and road-building
in the area. To mollify conservationists, it was proposed
that "all development activities be delayed for at least five
years to allow for a longer study of water quality and sedi-
mentation conditions occurring in the salmon spawning
beds. *The principal objective is to establish a base line of*

*data so that we may monitor any effects on the environ-
ment when development takes place."* [emphasis added]
As one conservationist put it, "What they mean is, 'at
least we'll be able to *measure* how badly we screw things
up.'"

Among the alternatives considered in the Forest Service study was wilderness management for all but a very
narrow corridor along existing roads—basically what conservationists had been proposing for years. This alternative was rejected, however, for two reasons: "unnecessary
loss of harvestable timber to meet the needs of the American people," and "the wilderness concept, as proposed by
the Wilderness Act, would be compromised because of
the proximity of the wilderness to roads and improvements."

But with incredibly twisted logic, the report states that
where road-building and logging would be carried out
close to the wilderness or primitive area boundaries,
"there should be very little effect on wilderness solitude
. . . the intrusion would be temporary noise; no appre-
ciable impact should occur."

Thus, quality of wilderness becomes a prime concern
of the Forest Service where it provides rationale for excluding a 20-mile-wide zone from wilderness designation
because of a road. But building roads and logging adjacent to existing wilderness has little or no impact.

With this final bit of evidence that the Forest Service
had no intentions of preserving the corridor, Senators
Church and Metcalf introduced a bill in the Senate in
August 1971 calling for wilderness designation of the
roadless portion of the corridor.

Too frequently it takes the mere stroke of an administrator's pen to set in motion the forces that would destroy

an area. To alter, to manipulate, to develop requires only
the flimsiest of excuses—economics. And once gone, wilderness is irretrievably lost.

To do nothing to land, however, to leave it untouched
and unimpaired, requires incredible justification, years of
studies and reviews and hearings, plus the efforts and
eternal vigilance of concerned citizens.

Rightly or wrongly, conservationists fear the Magruder
Corridor will witness the kinds of mistakes for which the
Forest Service has been severely criticized in other parts
of the Bitterroot National Forest and in other national
forests as well. In Congressional hearings last year, the
agency came under fire for the use of clear-cutting in
many areas where some foresters felt it was unjustified
and misapplied. More important than the clear-cutting
issue, however, was that these hearings underscored the
agency's increasing emphasis—some felt obsession—on
logging to the exclusion and detriment of other values.

Perhaps, as some suggest, the Forest Service has itself
become "overmature" and "decadent," and should be
replaced by a "young, vigorous growth" in the form of
a new, ecologically responsible and responsive agency.
Perhaps. But that will not occur soon enough to help re-
solve the Magruder Corridor issue.

The Church–Metcalf Bill must now go through the legislative mill of hearings, debate, and deliberation. Because of the concern of these two senators, there is cause
to be cautiously optimistic. However, passage in the
House is another matter. The corridor is included in an
Omnibus De Facto Wilderness Bill introduced by the
crusading conservationist from Pennsylvania, Representative John Saylor. But it faces stiff opposition from Idaho
Representative James McClure, in whose district the area

lies and who has been traditionally friendly to timber, mining, and other exploitative interests. He also sits on the House Interior and Insular Affairs Committee through which the bill must pass. Idaho's other Congressman, Orval Hansen, has criticized the Church–Metcalf Bill as being "premature."

The Magruder Corridor today is still lovely and wild, the Selway River continues to run sparkling clear. This controversy has become one of the longest ongoing battles in conservation annals, for seventeen years have elapsed since conservationists began discussions and initiated a proposal to the agency. One can only hope that the corridor can be added to the National Wilderness Preservation System, as seems right and proper, before another seventeen years pass.

# 6. Salmon Trip

Dusk is settling like a thin, gray veil over the Lemhi Valley's golden grass and stubbled green sage. We tool along a lonely stretch of highway. The Lemhi Mountains on the left are silhouetted against a darkening sky. To the right, the Beaverheads are tinged faint red by a dying sunset. We are on the trail of Lewis and Clark, 167 years late and seventy miles per hour too fast.

The little towns of Leadore and Lemhi and Tendoy flash by, wide spots in the road, populations 112 and who-knows-what, respectively. Bless the small towns, bless them all. Night falls at the town of Salmon. We gas up and check the trailer holding our folded raft.

We follow the Salmon River now, cross it once, twice, but it remains invisible in the blackness and the only world now is within the truncated cones of headlight on the asphalt ahead. At North Fork we turn left, leaving the main highway to follow that tortuous gravel road for forty miles, the road that parallels for a way the big river's

westward swing across Idaho. Problems right away. Someone has deemed it necessary to "improve" the road, which
means that it's all torn up now and likely to remain so
for a long time. *Progress*. Instead of a quarter of a million
dollars on this massive project, better to spend twenty-
five (single dollars, not million dollars) for a huge sign:

DANGER

EXTREMELY ROUGH AND DANGEROUS ROAD

NEXT 40 MILES.

TRAVEL AT YOUR OWN RISK

NO BODIES RECOVERED OR VEHICLES TOWED.

Joseph Wood Krutch said it all: "Rough roads act as
filters. The rougher the road, the finer the filter." Those
who care will make it.

Another hour and a half to the end of the road. The
whole body hums, jangled from the vibrations of a two
hundred and fifty mile drive. We throw our sleeping bags
on the ground and soon the river soothes and sings us to
sleep.

At dawn, we opt to skip breakfast in favor of getting
on the river as soon as possible. The big raft inflates
slowly, an oval shaped, neoprene serpent taking life. The
twenty-eight-foot length is far bigger than we really need
for just two people, me and Jim Campbell. Campbell is a
nuclear physicist-turned-river guide, investing his life sav-
ings in a labor of love. Smart man; knew what he wanted
out of life and neutrons weren't it. At this time the rest
of his rafts are in Hells Canyon with his partner, who is
running a group through that fabulous gorge.

The sun is still hidden behind steep hillsides as we

drift out into the main current. The river is broad and relatively shallow here, running along at a good pace. We pass through some small riffles, watching submerged rocks slip beneath us through the glass-clear water. In August the peak of runoff is passed and the river has settled into a normal, unsedimented flow. My thoughts go back to May on a trip in Hells Canyon where, upon reaching the confluence of the Salmon with the Snake, we found it a raging, coffee-colored torrent carrying huge trees ripped from shorelines upstream. Unfortunately, this trip won't take us all the way to the Snake. Our destination is only some 80 miles downstream—four days through some of the wildest and most beautiful country on earth.

The first rapid is Gunbarrel, a half hour after we start. Small, three- to four-foot waves. We get wet, but it presents no problems. Dodging rocks, we discover, is the main problem on the Salmon. There aren't any big water rapids as there are on the Colorado or in Hells Canyon, the kind that have fifteen-foot haystacks and holes that can swallow a twenty-eight-foot raft and spit it out upside down.

To make better time in the quiet stretches we row standing up, pushing first on one oar, then the other. The physical exercise feels good, though I would prefer just to let the current carry us along. I'm in no hurry. The country is magnificent, lush and green, tinged here and there with the amber of incipient fall. The land is parched and dry on the south-facing slopes, moist on the north. White beaches drift by. Around one bend we come upon a camp, a lean-to covered with a tarpaulin. A bald, bearded man stands by the shore, slowly scooping gravel into a sluice box with a bucket-like affair on the end of a stout pole. Bare to the waist, his rugged body is tanned the color of ponderosa bark. This is gold country, and if it has to be mined, I supposed this is the way to do it. He nods. We wave. A hardy soul, that man. May he never be replaced by a dredge or a bulldozer.

We are in wilderness now. On our right, on the north side of the river, is the Salmon River Breaks Primitive Area, a quarter of a million acres in size. On the left, the Idaho Primitive Area—1.2 million acres. Beyond the formal and artificial lines denoting these protected areas, there is an incredible amount of wild country. Over the high ridges to the north is the Selway River and farther on the Selway–Bitterroot Wilderness Area, another 1.2 million acres extending to the Lochsa River. From here to the Lochsa is a hundred and fifty rugged trail miles and the country has changed little since Lewis and Clark passed nearby. Up over the mountains looming above us on the south, it is another hundred and fifty miles to civilization. We float through the heart of a land—the size of the state of Connecticut—that is virgin wilderness. At least for a while.

You feel it. There is a wonderfully frightening sense of isolation. Looking downstream, I see ridge after high ridge receding into the distance, mountains that rise four, five thousand feet above us. Green, forested slopes, all unbroken. Around every bend a clear sparkling side stream tumbles down to join the Salmon and from every one of them you can dip a cup of cold, pure water.

These side streams are the life blood of the river, each one nourishing it and urging it on to its rendezvous with the Snake. Where the bigger creeks merge with the Salmon, there are rapids. Occasional flooding of these side streams has washed boulders into the main river channel and, raging against these constraints, the river is churned into foam.

We bounce through Ranier Rapid. The sun is high and hot, searing everything in the bottom of this deep gorge. Then Lantz Bar Rapid and Devil's Teeth. And Salmon Falls.

On the river one loses sense of time. Rather than a day being divided into arbitrary units of minutes or hours, time and life flow with the water here. Events are marked by significance rather than by numerals. There is clock time and there is river time and only river time is real. The other is some artificial measure we've allowed to dictate our lives. The clock tells us when to eat, when to make love, when to sleep. It dominates and stifles our education. At the ring of a bell we must shut off our minds to everything but mathematics. The result? A society tyrannized by watches and bells.

But river time is freedom.

On. More rapids the next day. Split Rock. Big Mallard. Elkhorn. Then some quiet stretches and we let the current carry us along. Campbell, what's happening to this country? Are you taking good care of it for me? For everyone? Yes, says he, but it's getting harder. Why? I ask, waving my hand to take in 2,000 square miles of wild country. What threats and disasters and dastardly deeds are we faced with here? A rhetorical question.

Campbell answers. There are too damn many people in this state, he says. And for a moment that sounds surprising, even funny. Idaho's population is about 700,000. Average population density is eight people per square mile. Room for lots more. But is there? Almost 70 percent of the state is public land, either National Forest or

Bureau of Land Management lands. Of the remainder, much of it is harsh and rugged country. Not at all conducive to supporting a large population. Unless you change it. Build dams, flatten hills, alter it to make it habitable. And then it wouldn't be Idaho.

Idaho is one of a handful of unspoiled states left in the nation. Should it be changed, developed, populated, industrialized? Suppose that the people of Idaho should suddenly realize that they don't want more people, pollution, and the lower quality of life that goes with growth. How do they stop it? Pass a law forbidding people to come here? No way. But suppose that some thought were given to real innovations in growth control. Like limiting services, for example. No more new roads. Setting a quota on electrical energy supplied to a given area. Or how about zoning by water availability. Limiting the amount of ground water tapped, or stored water distributed. Sorry, folks, we're fresh out of water here. You can come if you like, but we have no water for you. This last would be easiest to implement, for Idaho is largely arid.

Suppose also that the traditional thinking in industrial growth were changed and a new economic base were established. What base? How about a combination of agriculture and tourism? Agriculture is a desirable industry so long as it does not pollute or continue to expand at the expense of unspoiled land. Admittedly, it has a long way to go before reaching that state. DDT, herbicides, overgrazing, water development projects are all ways that farming contributes now to environmental degradation—but agriculture still means low population density. Tourism, controlled and regulated, can also be a desirable industry. The key, however, is in encouraging the right kind of tourism and discouraging the damaging kind.

Idaho's unique resource is unspoiled, wild country. To entice people here with the promise of golf courses, luxury hotels, motorized recreation, or Disneyland-type fun does injustice to the real beauty and peacefulness of the place. The more developments, the greater the impact on the wild beauty. Some day it may even be possible to free people from jobs which tie them to polluting factories. Maybe our society will move away from its consumptive, materialistic stage toward the arts, where products of the mind and hand will become more prized than products of the machine. Maybe.

Dreams. This is the kind of country that spawns such dreams, for the mind is free to match the wildness and expansiveness of the land. Perhaps the decline of a great civilization begins when it destroys the last of its wilderness.

Campbell and I drift on. The days on the river become a delirium of blazing sun, rocky walls, white and wild water, streams, forests, flowers, wilderness. I'll be back, I say. But I don't know for sure. I keep hoping above hope that nothing will change. But it will. And so will I. Someday I may not even need wilderness or a wild river. But somebody else will. Nice to think that it costs only a little love and care to pass on such treasures to another generation.

We drift on.

# A Guide to the Snake Wilderness

# Forest Service Wilderness and Primitive Areas

## Selway–Bitterroot Wilderness Area (1,240,600 acres)

*Locale:* North-central Idaho, overlapping into Montana. It is located SW of Missoula, and due W of Hamilton, Mont. The closest towns are Missoula and Hamilton on US 93.

*Description:* Contained within the area is the Bitterroot Mountain Range, high rugged alpine country. A large part of the drainage of the Selway and Lochsa Rivers is included within the Wilderness area. Heavily forested, it has large stands of ponderosa pine, Douglas fir, and alpine fir at higher elevations. Because of fires in the past, there are only a few stands of grand old cedars left, found mainly in stream bottoms. Major wildlife includes one of the largest herds of elk in the world. Deer, black bear, moose are also found. The southern part of the area contains the historic Nez Perce trail, the route used by the Indians to travel from Montana Valley to central and western Idaho. The elevations in this area range from 1,600 ft. on the Selway River to 10,000 ft. in the Bitterroot Mountains.

*Major Access:* Bitterroot Valley, Mont., US 93, and Lewis and Clark Highway, US 12, in Idaho. From access roads on all sides, trails go into the area.

*Climate:* There is a great variation in climate because of the variation in elevation. Be sure to take warm clothing when going into the high country, no matter how warm it is at river level. July and August are good months to visit.

*References:* Administered by the Bitterroot, Clearwater, and Nez Perce National Forests. Information on the area may be obtained from the U.S. Forest Service, Northern Region Headquarters, Federal Building, Missoula, Montana 59801.

*USGS Maps:* 1:250,000 Elk City, Idaho, and Hamilton, Mont. The entire area is now available in 7½′ size. The Index to topographic maps of Idaho lists these.

*Status:* This is the largest unit of the Forest Service's Wilderness System and was created in 1936. Seems to be adequately protected.

### Idaho Primitive Area (1,232,744 acres)

*Locale:* Geographic center of Idaho, contiguous to Salmon River Breaks Primitive Area on the north. Bounded on the north by Salmon River, on the east by the Bighorn Crags. Closest towns are Stanley on US 93. Further north is Challis on US 93. The western boundary may be reached from McCall on Idaho 55 via a gravel and dirt road to Yellow Pine.

*Description:* Beautiful and rugged, with varied terrain. There are high mountains, deeply incised canyons, dense forests and barren crags. The Middle Fork of the Salmon runs through the southeastern and eastern part of the area, and this gorge is among the deepest in North America, averaging more than 5,000 feet in depth. The Middle Fork was included in the Wild and Scenic Rivers Act of 1968. Indian petroglyphs and pictographs are found in many places. The Bighorn Crags near the eastern boundary are exceptionally spectacular, with jagged, eroded granite spires and peaks rising like surrealistic sculptures above transparent blue lakes. Wildlife is abundant and for many species the Primitive Area offers one of their last remaining habitats. There are bald and golden eagles, osprey, mountain sheep and goat, cougar, mule deer and whitetail deer, moose, fox, bobcat, lynx and numerous other permanent inhabitants. Rattlesnakes are numerous along the Middle Fork. Black bear are common, but no grizzlies have been reported. Man is the most dangerous species found here but fortunately is not a permanent resident.

*Major access:* There are 77 points of entry around the area. The Forest Service provides a descriptive brochure and map listing these points with additional information on access. Float trips are becoming distressingly popular on both the Middle Fork and the Main Salmon. An estimated several thousand people make the Middle Fork trip each year, and a limit may have to be set soon to minimize impact. Both trips require white water experience.

*References:* The area is administered by Boise, Challis, Payette, and Salmon National Forests, and lies within the Intermountain Region, U.S. Forest Service, Federal Office Building, Ogden, Utah 84401. Brochures and maps available from this address.

*USGS Maps:* quadrangle sheets not available for most of the area with the exceptions of De Costo, Big Creek, and Yellow Pine quadrangles. 1:250,000 scale maps available. Write: USGS, Federal Building, Denver, Colorado 80225. Forest Service maps showing trails are available from Intermountain Region office.

*Status:* The Forest Service seems to be preparing to delete large areas from both IPA and Salmon River Breaks. Idaho conservationists are not only preparing to fight such deletions, but are recommending additions totaling 264,000 acres to IPA and some 113,000 acres to

Salmon River Breaks. A big fight is shaping up. Love it or lose it.

## Salmon River Breaks Primitive Area (216,870 acres)

*Locale:* North side of the Salmon River, contiguous to the Idaho Primitive Area. Located between North Fork and Riggins, Idaho. Closest towns: North Fork (US 93), Elk City (Idaho 14), Riggins (US 95).

*Description:* This area is a very rugged terrain with heavily forested mountains (with "mature and overmature" timber, according to Forest Service literature) and steep riverbreak land. It is an important habitat for such wildlife as deer, elk, bear, bighorn sheep, mountain goat, and cougar. The fishing is excellent.

*Major access:* Access may be gained to the boundary from North Fork (US 93) by a rough road along the Salmon River canyon. Access may also be gained by raft, traveling the Salmon River downriver from North Fork. Idaho 13 and 14 goes from Grangeville to Elk City and from there a gravel, then dirt, road leads to the Primitive Area. There are several trails leading from the river to the interior.

*Climate:* Mild at river level so that the season can begin as early as April or May and last until October.

*References:* Administered by Bitterroot and Nez Perce National Forests. Write to Northern Regional Headquarters, Federal Bldg., Missoula, Montana 59801.

*USGS Maps:* 1:250,000 quadrangle map of Elk City, Idaho. No 15′ or 7½′ maps available.

*Status:* Hearings were to be held on whether to include this area in the wilderness system. The Forest Service does not seem to favor inclusion of a large part. It probably will recommend that the area revert to multiple use (read: logging and mining) unless hearings prove wilderness preservation is highly desired.

### Sawtooth Primitive Area (200,942 acres)

*Locale:* Central Idaho, south of the Idaho Primitive Area. Closest town: Stanley (US 93). On the west, Idaho 21 has now been extended from Lowman to Stanley, although winter travel on this road is uncertain, being subject to snowslides and washouts.

*Description:* The name Sawtooth Mountains aptly describes the type of peaks here—high, jagged, and toothlike. More than 170 alpine lakes and numerous streams make for a prodigious wildflower display. There are many excellent trails in the area, including the scenic Toxaway Loop Trail, which goes to several clear mountain lakes. If time is limited, the trail to Sawtooth Lake from the Iron Creek campground offers a good one-day sampling of what the Primitive Area has to offer. As in other Idaho wilderness sections, wildlife is abundant and varied.

*Major access:* A visitor's center at Redfish Lake, managed by the Sawtooth National Forest, provides up-to-date information on trails in the Primitive Area. There are numerous take-off points on all sides.

*Climate:* Access to the mountains is seldom possible before July. Good visiting months are July and August.

*References:* Administered by Boise, Challis, and Sawtooth National Forests. Write to Intermountain Regional Headquarters, Federal Office Bldg., Ogden, Utah 84401.

*USGS Maps:* 1:250,000 Hailey, Idaho, and Challis, Idaho, quadrangle maps. 30′ Bear Valley and Rocky Bar are listed but quite old and often erroneous.

*Status:* Hearings have been held on inclusion of the Sawtooth Primitive Area in the wilderness system. Renewed mining interest in the area offers a threat to wilderness status.

### Teton Wilderness Area (563,500 acres)

*Locale:* Northwestern Wyoming in the area between Yellowstone National Park and Grand Teton National Park. Closest town: Jackson, Wyoming, on US 89.

*Description:* This area, lying as it does with Grand Teton National Park to the south, Yellowstone National Park to the north, and the Washakie Wilderness area to the east, helps to form a vast, unspoiled wilderness area where it is possible to escape the tourist armies invading Grand Teton and Yellowstone national parks. A special interest spot is Two Ocean Pass, where Two Ocean Creek divides, one stream going to the Pacific and one stream to the Gulf of Mexico. The Teton Wilderness Area is summer range for the Jackson Hole elk herd, which winters at the National Elk Refuge outside Jackson.

*Major access:* Trails in the Teton Wilderness Area connect with trails in both Yellowstone and Grand Teton national parks as well as the Washakie Wilderness Area. The Teton Wilderness Area is easily accessible by trails on all sides.

*References:* Administered by Teton National Forest. Write to Intermountain Regional Headquarters, Federal Office Bldg., Ogden, Utah 84401.

*USGS Maps:* 1:250,000 Cody, Wyoming; Thermopolis, Wyoming, and Driggs, Idaho, quadrangles. 15′ Two Ocean Pass, and Mount Hancock, Wyoming. For the most part, the rest of the area is not mapped.

*Climate:* Winters can be ferocious. July and August are good visiting times.

*Status:* Not threatened because of its wilderness status.

# National Park Service Wilderness

## Yellowstone National Park (2,219,737 acres)

*Locale:* Northwest Wyoming. West entrance—West Yellowstone, Montana (US 191); North entrance—Gardiner, Montana (US 89); Northeast entrance—Silver Gate and Cooke City, Montana (US 12); East entrance —Cody, Wyoming (US 14, 20); South entrance—Jackson, Wyoming (US 89, 287).

*Description:* The tourist-oriented, bumper-to-bumper part of Yellowstone actually represents only a small percentage of the park area. Most of it is wilderness. And in this back country is located the wildlife you won't see next to Old Faithful—grizzly bears, bighorn sheep, large elk herds, and large bison herds, moose, pronghorn antelope, possibly a wolf and foxes, bald eagles and ospreys. There are petrified forests and geyser basins. And no tourists. Some of the most beautiful lakes (Heart Lake, for example) are in the wild areas but readily accessible by trails. The trails to Shoshone Lake are recommended. In the southwestern corner of the park, the trail into Bechler meadows and along the Bechler River is good for both scenery and wildlife.

*Major Access:* (Described above.) There are 1,000 miles of trails in the back country of Yellowstone. File an itinerary with the park rangers first; get a fire permit.

*Climate:* The winters are long and hard. While the park opens about the end of May, don't plan on any extensive backpacking much before the end of June. The autumn is a beautiful time of the year in the park, but beware of sudden snows.

*References:* Administered by the National Park Service. Write to the Superintendent, Yellowstone National Park, Wyoming 82190.

*USGS Maps:* Special map of Yellowstone National Park available, scale 2 mi. to the inch.

*Status:* The major threat to wilderness in the National Parks comes from the Park Service itself when it succumbs to outside pressure to "open the locked-up" areas to the omniverous automobile. There is no doubt that Yellowstone is over-crowded and the situation must be alleviated. Yet to build more roads into the wilderness here defeats the very purpose of the park. A better system would be to have visitors park their cars outside and take sightseeing buses into the park.

### Grand Teton National Park (300,000 acres)

*Locale:* Northwest Wyoming, to the south of Yellowstone National Park. Closest town: Jackson, Wyoming, on US 187, 89, 26.

*Description:* Tall, jagged mountains rise abruptly from Jackson Hole. The park is crowded, and getting more crowded each year during the summer, but by expending a little energy you can still escape too much humanity. The trail from Cascade Canyon to Death Canyon through Alaska Basin gives a taste of everything the park has to offer—wildflower-carpeted meadows, cascading mountain streams and waterfalls, high mountain vistas, dense evergreen forests, alpine tundra. Backcountry use is exploding in the Tetons. Lake Solitude has become Lake Multitude. Firewood is now nonexistent at some of the high elevation campsites. Primus or butane stoves are an ecological necessity nowadays for backpackers and climbers in order to minimize their impact. The Park Service may be forced to begin rationing backcountry use here. As a first step, a program should be started to phase out the use of horses, whose impact is far greater than that of hikers. Ultimately, restrictions on backpackers and climbers may be necessary.

As one would suspect, the wildlife is both abundant and varied—deer, moose, elk, bighorn sheep, bears, pronghorn, pika, coyote. More than 200 species of birds have been recorded in the park—bald eagle, trumpeter swan, and white pelicans included. Climbers consider the Teton Range a favorite area because of the variety of climbs and the hard rock. It is, in fact, becoming the climbing center of the country.

*Major Access:* There are well-established trails into most remote areas of the park. Some are open for only a few weeks each year because of snow conditions, so check with the rangers first.

*Climate:* From June through September the days are pleasant and the nights cold. Expect a thunderstorm, sometimes with snow, almost every afternoon in July and August.

*References:* Administered by the National Park Service. Write to Superintendent, Grand Teton National Park, Moose, Wyoming 83012.

*USGS Maps:* A special map of Grand Teton National Park is available, scale 1 mi. per inch.

*Status:* All of the high Teton country seems certain

of wilderness designation. However, conservationists fear that the Park Service plans to exclude some of the lovely valley lands and lakes, such as Leigh, Bradley, and Taggart lakes. Conservationists also recommended a wilderness boundary placed one-quarter mile offshore on the west side of Jackson Lake to keep that rugged and wild shoreline free of speedboats.

## Craters of the Moon National Monument
### (53,545 acres)

*Locale:* Off highway, US Alt. 93, 20, 26. Closest town: Arco, Idaho, on US Alt. 93, 26, twenty miles from the Monument.

*Description:* Great lava eruptions thousands of years ago covered the landscape with black stone-like lava flows. Virtually the entire eighty-three square miles of the Monument is wilderness, the only exception being a seven-mile loop road with several side nature trails. Great and small caves and caverns abound in the area. Although at first glance there appears to be little or no vegetation, more than 200 species of plants flourish in the area, and a minor miracle occurs every spring when the barren cinder cones are covered with carpets of magenta dwarf monkeyflowers and yellow dwarf buckwheat. An ancient Indian trail goes through the area, and remnants of the temporary stone shelters built by the Indians can still be seen.

*Major Access:* There are points of interest off the developed tourist trails, but a trip into the trailless lava should not be lightly undertaken. Check with the ranger at Monument Headquarters for suggestions. Good heavy hiking boots are an absolute must.

*Climate:* Very cold and snowy in winter, hot in summer. Good visiting months are June through September.

*References:* Administered by the National Park Service. Write for information to Superintendent, Craters of the Moon National Monument, Box 29, Arco, Idaho 83213.

*USGS Maps:* Special Map of Craters of the Moon National Monument available, scale: ½ mile to 1 inch.

*Status:* Protected.

# De Facto Wilderness

## Western Tetons

*Locale:* Directly west of and contiguous to Grand Teton National Park. Adjacent to the Idaho-Wyoming border. Closest towns: Driggs and Victor, Idaho, on Idaho 33.

*Description:* This remote area deserves to belong to Grand Teton National Park. Ecologically, geologically, and historically, the bonds to the park are incontestable. Only a political boundary says that it is not a part of the National Park. The scenery is every bit as spectacular. The western Tetons comprise a region of some 200,000 acres of prime wilderness, containing beautiful canyons, cirques and basins with magnificent forests, wonderful free-flowing streams, and alpine hillsides that burst forth with some of the finest wildflower displays to be seen in the entire Teton range. There are mule deer, elk, moose, black bear, bobcat, cougar, and coyote. Occasionally a grizzly bear is seen in the northern region. The area is important historically. It was from the summit of Table

Mountain that the pioneer western photographer, William Henry Jackson, made the first photographs of Grand Teton in 1872. Teton Valley, Idaho, formerly called Pierre's Hole, was the site of the fur trappers' rendezvous in 1832. Conant Pass to the north and Phillips and Teton Passes to the south were common routes across the Teton Range for both fur trappers and Indians. The major canyons contain Douglas fir, Englemann Spruce, lodgepole pine, and aspen. The high country basins contain limber pine and alpine fir. The trail from Cascade Canyon to Death Canyon in Grand Teton National Park travels through Alaska Basin, which is outside the Park and in this western Teton area.

*Major access:* This area is more easily reached from the Idaho side than from the Wyoming (Grand Teton National Park) side. Nearly every major canyon is penetrated by roads which provide reasonable access to the trail heads. These trails on the Idaho side connect with trails in the park to form an excellent hiking network through prime wilderness.

*Climate:* From late June to early September the weather is good with warm days and cold nights. Again, as with Grand Teton National Park, summer afternoon thundershowers are to be expected.

*References:* Administered by the Targhee National Forest under the multiple-use concept. Write to Supervisor, Targhee National Forest, St. Anthony, Idaho 83445.

*USGS Maps:* 1:250,000 Driggs, Idaho, quadrangle. 7½′ Clawson and McRenolds Reservoir, Idaho, quadrangles.

*Status:* The Idaho Alpine Club formally asked the Forest Service to conduct a wilderness study on some 180,000 acres of the Western Tetons. The study was in the process at press time. Although the Service had agreed to a moratorium on logging and other developments within the study area, virtually all trails are still open to the destructive motorized intrusions of trail bikes in summer and snowmobiles in winter.

## Big Desert Lava Beds

*Locale:* West of Idaho Falls, Blackfoot, and Pocatello on the Snake River Plain in Idaho. There are several areas of lava beds. One unit (200,000 acres) is directly southwest, south, and east of Craters of the Moon National Monument. Another, off US 20 in the triangle formed by US 20, 26 and US 26, 91, is approximately 46,000 acres.

*Description:* The lava beds, of varying ages, offer a forbidding and convoluted landscape. They are roadless because building a road through this difficult terrain would be very expensive and beset by many technical difficulties. This is one case where wilderness designation might be fairly easy to attain, mainly because no one has yet found a "use" for lava beds—you can't farm 'em, graze 'em, or mine 'em. Thank heavens. Here is an ecological system that is unique and far from barren. In the older flows typical plant life includes cactus, juniper trees, sagebrush. In the north-south crevasses, because they get more sunlight, grow such desert plants as cactus. The east-west crevasses support moisture-loving plants such as ferns. Coyote and cougar, as well as the smaller rodents and rattlesnakes, are in the areas.

*Major access:* As mentioned in the section on Craters of the Moon National Monument, a hiking trip into lava country must never be attempted lightly. To begin with, walking on the jagged lava with its deep crevasses and holes is extremely difficult. Then, too, it is desert country and reliable water sources are generally non-existent. Sturdy boots, water, compass, and a hiking companion are heartily recommended. If you're a lava flow neophyte and just want a taste of the country, it is possible to stick to the major highways and just walk a few hundred yards into the lavas. It isn't wilderness, but it may inspire you to go on to the real thing.

*Climate:* The lava beds are extremely cold in winter and hot in summer. Winter temperatures can range to 40 below zero while summer temperatures may go above 100° F. The spring wildflowers are usually abundant in late June.

*References:* The lava beds are administered by the Bureau of Land Management, with headquarters in Boise, Idaho.

*USGS Maps:* 1:250,000 Idaho Falls, Idaho, quadrangle. The lava area near Idaho Falls is covered by 7½' maps.

*Status:* No major clamor is currently being made to make the lava beds part of the wilderness system.

### Centennial Mountains

*Locale:* About 80 miles due north of Idaho Falls, 25 miles due west of Yellowstone National Park on the Idaho-Montana border. The closest towns are Humphrey on US 91 and West Yellowstone, Montana, on US 191 and 20.

*Description:* While these are relatively low mountains —nothing over 10,000 feet—the area has forested canyons and several small lakes and streams. The headwaters of Camus Creek and other streams that eventually sink into the lavas further to the south spring from the Centennial Mountains. The Continental Divide runs down the middle of the mountains. Moose and elk have their habitat here.

*Major Access:* On the Idaho side trails follow the numerous creeks. There are very few trails on the Montana side, however. The Red Rock Lakes National Wildlife Refuge boundary comes to the edge of the mountains on the Montana side.

*Climate:* July and August are the best months to visit the Centennials, since deep snows are possible at other times.

*References:* The Montana side of the Centennials is under the jurisdiction of the Bureau of Land Management, headquartered at Billings, Montana, while the Idaho side is in the Targhee National Forest, headquartered at St. Anthony, Idaho 83445.

*USGS Maps:* 1:250,000 Ashton, Idaho, quadrangle. 15′ Lower Red Rock Lake and Upper Red Rock Lake, Idaho, quadrangles.

*Status:* Conservationists want to see the Centennials become part of the wilderness system—but so far there has been no widely publicized effort.

## White Cloud Mountains

*Locale:* West of Sawtooth Valley, Idaho. Nearest towns: Stanley (US 93) and Clayton (US 93).

*Description:* See Chapter 4.

*Major Access:* A road goes along the East Fork of the Salmon River, from which you can pick up a trail that follows Little Boulder Creek. This trail branches in about six miles, the southwest branch traveling by Castle Peak, the north branch flowing to the Boulder Chain Lakes and Frog Lake.

*Climate:* As with most high mountain country, the snow flies early and stays late. July and August are good hiking months. Mosquitoes love these months, too.

*References:* The White Cloud Peaks lie in the Challis National Forest. Headquarters: Challis, Idaho 83226.

*USGS Maps:* 1:250,000 Challis, Idaho, quadrangle. 7½′ Boulder Chain lakes.

*Status:* See Chapter 4.

## Boulder Mountains

*Locale:* South of the White Cloud Mountains on the Custer County–Blaine County line, northeast of US 93 in Idaho. Nearest town: Ketchum, Idaho (US 93).

*Description:* Another beautiful and practically unknown high mountain area with peaks of 10,000 and 11,000 feet. Several creeks which flow into the Big Wood River have their headwaters here. Historically, the area was the site of boom and bust gold and silver mining. In the Boulder Mountains, as in the Pioneer and Sawtooth Mountains, great glaciers have been responsible for sculpting the mountains into steep cirques and U-shaped canyons. Typical tree species are Ponderosa pine, lodgepole pine, Douglas fir, Engelmann spruce, alpine fir, and whitebark pine. Deer, elk, mountain goat, and bighorn sheep are found in the area.

*Major Access:* There are many trails in the range, some starting from dirt roads off US 93. The Boulder mountains are well linked by trails with the southern White Clouds.

*Climate:* July and August are the best months for visits. There are many good ski-touring possibilities in the Boulders, and spring ski-touring is quite popular.

*References:* Administered by the Sawtooth National Forest, headquartered at Twin Falls, Idaho 83301.

*USGS Maps:* 1:250,000 Hailey, Idaho, quadrangle.

*Status:* Included by conservationists in the Greater Sawtooth National Park and Recreation Area proposal.

## Pioneer Mountains

*Locale:* Southeast of the Boulder Mountains. Southeast of Trail Creek road which goes from Ketchum, Idaho (US 93), to Alt. US 93 near Mackay, Idaho. Closest town: Ketchum, Idaho (US 93).

*Description:* Hyndman Peak is the tallest mountain in the range at 12,078 feet. Devils Bedstead and Standhope Peak are other spectacularly beautiful mountains. Antelope, deer, and elk are found in the area. This area is part of the vast mountainous network formed by the White Clouds, Boulders, and Pioneers, with spectacular views, wildflowers, wildlife.

*Major Access:* There are several trails and access roads going into the Pioneers. A road off the Trail Creek road following the East Fork of the Big Lost River branches and follows Wild Horse Creek. There is a campground on this road which makes it a good base for reaching Hyndman Peak.

*Climate:* Typically, Idaho high country winters start in September and end in June. The flat arid valleys around can be very hot in summer, very cold in winter.

*References:* Administered by the Sawtooth National Forest, headquartered at Twin Falls, Idaho 83301, and the Challis National Forest, headquartered at Challis, Idaho 83226.

*USGS Maps:* 1:250,000 Hailey, Idaho, and Idaho Falls, Idaho, quadrangles.

*Status:* Recommended by conservationists for inclusion in the Greater Sawtooth National Park and Recreation Area proposal.

### Smoky Mountains

*Locale:* South of Galena summit (on US 93), west of Ketchum, Idaho. Closest town: Ketchum, Idaho (US 93).

*Description:* The Smoky Mountains are located on the southwest side of the Big Wood River and its streams contribute to this river's flow. The peaks are in the 9,000- and 10,000-foot range and are heavily forested. Historically, they were the scene of early mining attempts, as were other mountains in the area of Ketchum. Deer, elk, and other large Northern Rocky Mountain wildlife abound here.

*Major Access:* Many trails go into the area from roads jutting off US 93.

*Climate:* July and August are best. The early fall can be lovely with clear, warm days and frosty nights, but because of the snow possibilities it is best to stay in the lower country.

*References:* Administered by the Sawtooth National Forest, headquartered at Twin Falls, Idaho 83301.

*USGS Maps:* 1:250,000 Hailey, Idaho, quadrangle.

*Status:* Recommended by conservationists for inclusion in the Greater Sawtooth National Park and Recreation Area.

## Lost River Range

*Locale:* Northeast of the stretch of Alt. US 93 going from Arco to Challis, Idaho. Nearest towns: Challis, Arco, and Mackay, Idaho, all on US Alt. 93.

*Description:* The Lost River Range lies in a drier portion of the country than do the Sawtooth Mountains, so they are not as heavily forested. The highest point in Idaho, Mt. Borah (12,655 ft.), is in this range. On the Southwest side the range towers over the arid Big Lost River Valley with no intervening foothills, making for very spectacular scenery. There are mountain goats, elk, deer, and antelope in the lower flats.

*Major Access:* Two roads cut across the range; the north road extends from Dickey to Goldberg and the southerly one goes through Pass Creek Gorge over Pass Creek summit to the road connecting May and Howe. There are some trails into the range; most of them start on the northeast side of the range from Pahsimeroi Valley.

*Climate:* The high mountain peaks get much snow and wind in the winter, while the surrounding valleys are extremely hot in the summer.

*References:* Administered by Challis National Forest, headquartered at Challis, Idaho 83226.

*USGS Maps:* 1:250,000 Dubois, Idaho, quadrangle. 15′ Doublespring, Donkey Hills, and Hawley Mt. quadrangles cover portions of the range.

*Status:* No permanent protection from the horrors of mining, timbering, and so on, yet available.

## Lemhi Range

*Locale:* Lies between the Pahsimeroi Valley (road going from Howe to May) and the Lemhi Valley (Idaho 28). Closest towns: May and Patterson on the May-Howe road and Leadore on Idaho 28.

*Description:* High mountain peaks rise abruptly from the Lemhi Valley side, but there are intervening hills from the Pahsimeroi Valley side. There are many antelope herds in the Pahsimeroi Valley. The land below the range can be viewed from the Patterson Creek Trail on the Pahsimeroi side. On the Lemhi Valley side, several ghost mining towns lie in the shadow of the mountains, one of them being Gilmore. From Gilmore a road goes to Meadow Lake campground, a beautiful high alpine lake all too popular with Idahoans. Diamond Peak is rather popular with mountain climbers. It is a surprisingly rugged and little known country.

*Major Access:* Many trails go into the range from both sides.

*Climate:* High country is often not accessible until July because of the heavy winter snows. The Pahsimeroi Valley is hot in the summer.

*References:* Administered by Salmon National Forest (headquarters, Salmon, Idaho 83467), Challis National Forest (headquarters, Challis, Idaho 83226) and Targhee National Forest (headquarters, St. Anthony, Idaho 83445).

*USGS Maps:* 1:250,000 Dubois, Idaho, quadrangle. 15′ quadrangles available for the area.

*Status:* No permanent protection yet available from mining and timbering. A large number of claims for thorium and rare earth deposits have been staked in the area. Speculators are gambling that AEC development of breeder reactors will bring a boom in thorium. It will also devastate these lovely mountains.

### Magruder Corridor

*Locale:* Between the Salmon River Breaks Primitive Area and the Selway-Bitterroot Wilderness Area. Closest town: Elk City on Idaho 14 and North Fork on US 93.

*Description:* See Chapter 5.

*Major Access:* A very primitive road goes into the corridor from Darby, Montana, on US 93. The old Nez Perce trail can be picked up from the road about one-third of the way from Magruder Ranger Station to Paradise Hills Ranger Station. Other trails include one up Indian Creek and one up White Cap Creek, both of which go to the heart of the Selway-Bitterroot Wilderness Area. Another trail from the Paradise Ranger Station follows the Selway River downstream.

*Climate:* Along the Selway River the climate is quite mild and moist because of the low elevation. The higher country and mountains are typical cold Rocky Mountain climate.

*References:* Administered by Nez Perce National Forest (headquarters, Grangeville, Idaho 83530) and Bitterroot National Forest (headquarters, Hamilton, Montana 59840).

*USGS Maps:* 1:250,000 Elk City, Idaho, quadrangle. 7½′ quadrangle maps available for parts of the area.

*Status:* See Chapter 5.

## Hells Canyon

*Locale:* This is the canyon formed by the Snake River on the Idaho-Oregon border. The canyon itself is more than 100 miles long, although not all of it is free-flowing because of dams. Closest towns: Riggins, Idaho (US 95); New Meadows, Idaho (US 95); Enterprise, Oregon (Ore. 3); Baker, Oregon (US 30); Imnaha, Oregon.

*Description:* See Chapter 3.

*Major Access:* There is a road down to Dug Bar by way of the Imnaha River. A road goes to Pittsburgh Landing from the area of Whitebird, Idaho. There are trails on both the Oregon and Idaho sides of the river with the exception of the last five or six miles below Hells Canyon dam. There are no trails in this stretch. The Seven Devils Mountains have numerous trails, and several trails go from the high country down into the canyon, e.g., Granite Creek and Bernard Creek. There is a road to the lookout at Hat Point with trails from there down to the river through several side canyons. A road goes into the Seven Devils Ranger Station from US 95 south of Riggins.

*Climate:* Very mild at river level with frequently snowless winters. Very hot in the summer. The high country has typical alpine winters with snow until May or June.

*References:* Administered by the Wallowa-Whitman National Forest on the Oregon side (headquarters, Baker, Ore. 97814) and Payette National Forest (headquarters, McCall, Idaho 83638) and Nez Perce National Forest (headquarters, Grangeville, Idaho 83530) on the Idaho side.

*USGS Maps:* 1:250,000 Baker, Grangeville, and Pullman quadrangles. The area has been well mapped by 7½' and 15' quadrangles. There is also a USGS Special Map of the Lower Snake River.

*Status:* See Chapter 3.

## Salt River Range

*Locale:* East of Starr Valley, Wyoming (US 89). Closest town: Freedom, Wyoming (US 89). Boundaries are the Snake River on the north, Star Valley and the Salt River to the west, and Greys River on the east.

*Description:* Contains the headwaters and principal drainages of the Salt and Greys rivers. There are several high mountains and the range merges to the east with the Wyoming Range, which is another potential wilderness area. The highest peak is 10,763-foot Rock Lake Peak. Fishing is reported to be excellent.

*Major Access:* The Fire Trail runs about fifty miles along the length of the Range. It begins at the Forks of Greys River campground and comes out on the gravel road cutoff between Smoot and Big Piney. Many other trails take off from the Fire Trail.

*Climate:* Cold and snowy in winter. July and August are good hiking months.

*References:* Administered by the Bridger National Forest, headquartered at Kemmerer, Wyoming 83101.

*USGS Maps:* 1:250,000 Driggs, Idaho, quadrangle. 30' Afton, Wyo., quadrangle. 7½' Stewart Peak, Wyo., quadrangle.

*Status:* Needs to be studied as a possible wilderness area.

## Gros Ventre Range

*Locale:* Southeast of Jackson Hole, Wyoming. North of the Hoback River in Wyoming. Closest town: Jackson, Wyoming (US 89, 26, 187).

*Description:* In back of Sheep Mountain (Sleeping Indian), southeast of Jackson Hole, lies a land of high mountains, deep canyons, and clear streams. It is excellent backpacking country. Some of the spectacular parts are Turquoise Lake in upper Granite Creek, Shoal Creek with a hundred foot waterfall, 11,645-foot Darwin Peak, and Jazz Creek with high open meadows. Wildflowers are abundant. There are bighorn sheep, moose, and elk. Fishing is excellent. The headwaters of the Gros Ventre River are in this range. It is good ski-touring country, too.

*Major Access:* The Gros Ventre Range is easily accessible by way of Granite Creek. A road runs off US 189 and 187 as far up as Granite Hot Springs, and the campground there makes a good base camp. Another point of interest is the Gros Ventre Slide Geological Area, where the north end of Sheep Mountain slid into the Gros Ventre River in 1925 and formed a lake.

*Climate:* Same old mountain weather—cold in winter, pleasant in July and August.

*References:* Mostly in the Teton National Forest, headquartered at Jackson, Wyoming 73001; the eastern section is in Bridger National Forest, headquartered at Kemmerer, Wyoming 83101.

*USGS Maps:* 1:250,000 Driggs, Idaho quadrangle. Partially covered by 7½′ Grizzly Lake, Upper Slide Lake, Burnt Mt., Wyoming, quadrangles.

*Status:* Senator Clifford Hansen has introduced in the

U.S. Senate a bill to give the area wilderness status. The area (145,550 acres) would include most of the roadless country between the Gros Ventre and Hoback Rivers, between the Bridger-Teton interface boundary and Sheep Mountain.

# Wildlands adjacent to the Snake Region

## Eagle Cap Wilderness Area (220,416 acres)

*Locale:* Northeastern Oregon. Closest towns: Enterprise on Oregon 82, Le Grande, Oregon (US 30), and Lewiston-Clarkston (on the Idaho-Oregon border) are the largest towns near the Wilderness Area.

*Description:* The highest peaks in eastern Oregon loom over the deep canyons of the Eagle Cap Wilderness Area. Of these, the highest is Sacajawea with an elevation of 10,033 ft. This mountain, along with the Matterhorn and Eagle Cap, is a favorite haunt of mountain climbers. The Matterhorn has the added distinction of being composed of shimmering blue-white limestone. The mountains are mostly bare on the top steep slopes. Alpine fir occurs near meadows further down the slopes, and Engelmann spruce, Douglas fir, and white fir are found in the canyons. More than fifty lakes in the area provide good fishing along with beautiful scenery. Adjacent to the area, to the northwest, is the 80,000-acre proposed addition to the Eagle Cap in the Minam River drainage.

*Major access:* A good jumping-off point into the area

is Wallowa Lake. Trails which start into the interior from all sides of the lake are generally good.

*Climate:* Good weather in July and August. Snow likely before and after.

*References:* Administered by Wallowa-Whitman National Forest. Write for information from Pacific Northwest Regional Headquarters, P. O. Box 3623, 319 SW Pine St., Portland, Oregon 97208.

*USGS Maps:* 15′ Cornucopia, Eagle Cap, Enterprise, Joseph (Oregon) quadrangles available.

*Status:* Not threatened because of its wilderness status.

### Jarbidge Wilderness Area (64,667 acres)

*Locale:* Northeastern Nevada near the Nevada-Idaho border. Nearest town, Jarbidge, reached from a secondary road from Deeth, off Interstate 80.

*Description:* This very remote section of Nevada is noted for its wildlife and for the Jarbidge Mountain Range with eight peaks whose altitudes range from 10,-000 to 11,000 ft. Fishing is good in the streams. The area is largely forested, with bare mountain tops giving way to alpine fir and then to aspen and occasional mountain mahogany. The wildflowers are at their best in the meadows during July and August.

*Major access:* There are not many trails in the area. Check with the Forest Service for trails good for scenery or for fishing.

*Climate:* July and August best.

*References:* Administered by Humboldt National Forest. Write for information to Intermountain Regional Headquarters, Federal Office Bldg., Ogden, Utah 84401.

*USGS Maps:* 15′ Jarbidge quadrangle available. Write to USGS for information on the latest maps.

*Status:* Not threatened because of its wilderness designation.

## Bruneau-Owyhee De Facto Wilderness

*Locale:* Southwestern Idaho, and southeastern Oregon and part of northern Nevada. Closest towns: Bruneau on Idaho 51 and Jordan Valley, Oregon, on US 95.

*Description:* This is a region of several million acres embracing desert, canyon, and arid mountain country. Largely Bureau of Land Management land. The Owyhee and Malheur River canyons are colorful and spectacular. Wildlife in the region includes antelope and a small herd of desert bighorn sheep in the mountains. A point of special interest is Bruneau Canyon. After coming across flat, sparse, desert land, the earth suddenly is ripped open into a gorge 2,000 feet deep in places where the Bruneau River has cut into the basaltic rock. Very winding, very steep, very impressive.

*Major Access:* There are a few dirt roads and no formal trails as such. Because this is desert land, desert precautions must be observed when striking out across country.

*Climate:* Hot in the summer; spring and fall are good visiting months.

*References:* This land is mostly under the jurisdiction of the Bureau of Land Management, headquartered in Boise, Idaho 83701.

*USGS Maps:* 1:250,000 Jordan Valley, Idaho, and Twin Falls, Idaho, quadrangles; also McDermitt and Wells, Nevada, quadrangles. Bruneau Canyon is covered by 15′ Bruneau and Winter Camp quadrangles.

*Status:* Because there are roads lacing the several million acres, only about 200,000 acres could possibly be considered for wilderness designation. However, an extensive study should be made.

### St. Joe-Mallard-Larkins De Facto Wilderness

*Locale:* Southwest of Superior, Montana (on Interstate 90). Due east of Clarkia on Idaho 3. Closest town: Clarkia, Idaho (Idaho 3).

*Description:* This area has many clear lakes and streams and the fishing is excellent. The main reason these 150,000 acres have remained untouched and roadless is that much of the area was burned over in 1910 and the trees have not yet grown to commercial size. Even so, it has dense stands of fir and cedar, some of the cedar being five feet thick. Mud Lake, surprisingly, is a beautiful blue in the midst of the green spruce and mountain hemlock. There are twelve small lakes within four miles of Larkin's Peak. Heart Lake is located almost 800 feet below Heart Pass; this 300-acre lake has only about 300 feet of shore line because of almost vertical granite cliffs surrounding it. There are mountain goats on the rocky peaks, and the area is habitat also for large herds of deer and elk.

*Major Access:* The area is easily accessible by roads through Clarkia and Headquarters, Idaho, and through Red Ives Ranger Station, Montana. There are trails going to the lake area.

*Climate:* Mild in the lowland areas. Not so mild in the higher mountains.

*References:* Administered by St. Joe National Forest, headquartered at St. Maries, Idaho 83861; and the Clearwater National Forest, headquartered at Orofino, Idaho 83544.

*USGS Maps:* 1:250,000 Hamilton, Mont., quadrangle. 7½′ Buzzard Roost, Idaho, and Mallard Peak quadrangles cover part of the area.

*Status:* The Forest Service has proposed 70,000 acres of only the higher peaks for inclusion in a "Pioneer" area. Conservationists have proposed 150,000 acres including lowland areas as well, and want it maintained as a true wilderness area.

# Acknowledgments I

The author would like to express his thanks to the United States Forest Service, the Bureau of Reclamation, the U. S. Army Corps of Engineers, the Idaho Water Resources Board, several power companies, lumber companies and real estate developers, chambers of commerce, such organizations as the Idaho Mining Association and the Society of American Foresters, and countless businessmen and industrialists, all of whom, collectively and individually, have made this book not only possible but absolutely necessary.

# Acknowledgments II

No book is the sole work of one person and this book especially owes much to many people.

First there are old friends and hiking companions in Idaho who, between battles to stave off the developers, managed to find time to offer comments on the manuscript: Pete Henault, the untiring president of the Hells Canyon Preservation Council; Russ Brown, president of the Greater Sawtooth Preservation Council and perhaps the one person who has been largely responsible for keeping the White Clouds mineless; Jerry Jayne, the incredible president of the Idaho Environmental Council and my candidate for the hardest working (and most effective) volunteer conservationist in the nation.

Jim Campbell and Hank Miller, founders and operators of Wilderness Encounters, deserve special thanks for their help. Doris Milner and G. M. Brandborg of Hamilton, Montana, were especially helpful in preparing the Magruder Corridor chapter. I should also like to thank Floyd Harvey of Lewiston, Idaho, with whom I made my early Hells Canyon trips. Dick and Sue Miller offered helpful comments on the history of the Snake country.

There are many others, perhaps too numerous to mention here, who shared campfires and ideas with me. I would like to single out two people for their years of friendship and contagious enthusiasm for wilderness: Al and Lee McGlinsky. Many of their thoughts and feelings are in this book.

Thanks, also, to Les Line, editor of Audubon Magazine, which published some of my early writings and pictures on the Snake country, and to Stewart Udall, who was kind enough to spend an evening here, during a busy schedule, to offer some historical perspective on the early Hells Canyon fight.

Many thanks go to Barbara Holliday of Senator Bob Packwood's office for her tireless efforts. And my special gratitude goes to Senator Bob Packwood himself. For caring. For not only caring, but for fighting hard for a place we both love: Hells Canyon. His commitment to saving wild and beautiful places is both deep and sincere.

Many, many others contributed to this book indirectly: Idaho Governor Cecil Andrus; Sam Day, fiery editor of the Intermountain Observer; Senator Frank Church (we've had our differences as to methods, but I know his feelings are just as strong), and Ernie Day and Mort Brigham and H. Tom Davis and Bill Hall and a host of others. All share an increasing concern over the quality of life and the future of Idaho. And they are doing something about it. As a de facto citizen of that state (I shall return), I appreciate their efforts.

And finally I must make special note of the patience, understanding, and encouragement of my lovely wife, Barbara. In a very real sense this book is hers too, through the sharing of many adventures and through her own valuable research. The guide portion of this book, covering de facto and statutory wilderness in the Snake River drainage, is entirely her work.

*B.N./July, 1972/Evergreen, Colorado*

# About the Author

Boyd Norton, a former research physicist and technical director at the Atomic Energy Commission's National Reactor Testing Station in Idaho, has been an active conservationist for more than a decade. He was a founder of the Hells Canyon Preservation Council, the Idaho Environmental Council and the Greater Sawtooth Preservation Council. Mr. Norton now devotes full time to writing and photography. His words and pictures have appeared in such magazines as *Life, Audubon, Smithsonian,* and *American Heritage,* and he has contributed to a number of books, including *America the Beautiful* and *Wildflowers of the Mountains.*

Mr. Norton now resides in Evergreen, Colo., in a mountain hideaway with his wife and two children.

## DATE DUE

| MAR 1 6 1988 | | | |
|---|---|---|---|
| | | | |
| | | | |
| | | | |
| | | | |
| | | | |
| | | | |
| | | | |
| | | | |
| | | | |
| | | | |
| | | | |
| | | | |
| | | | |
| | | | |
| | | | |
| | | | |
| | | | |
| GAYLORD | | | PRINTED IN U.S.A. |